GREGG SPEED STUDIES

BY

JOHN ROBERT GREGG

THE GREGG PUBLISHING COMPANY

NEW YORK CHICAGO SAN FRANCISCO

CONTENTS

FOUNDATIONS OF SPEED AND ACCURACY

TITLES OF ARTICLES IN SHORTHAND

METHODS OF HANDLING

SPEED STUDIES is readily adaptable to three general methods of use. Preceding the work under any of the plans, however, a thorough study should be made of "Foundations of Speed and Accuracy."

First Plan. The first plan contemplates the use of SPEED STUDIES simultaneously with the GREGG SHORTHAND MANUAL, a corresponding lesson in SPEED STUDIES being assigned with each Manual lesson. This plan probably will secure the most satisfactory results, as it makes possible early dictation, and a complete welding of theory with practice.

Second Plan. With the second plan, GREGG SPEED STUDIES is intended to be introduced after the student has completed the GREGG SHORTHAND MANUAL, the aim being to use the early "speed studies" and drills as a review. Emphasis should be placed upon the reading and dictation drills provided in the shorthand plates.

Third Plan. In the third plan, the material presented in the "studies" and the executional drills contained in the first eight lessons, may be introduced as supplementary material to the Manual. From Study VIII on to XXI the work may be concentrated wholly on the reading and dictation material in the shorthand plates, and the "studies" held for convenient assignments with the dictation material contained in Studies XXI–XXX after the GREGG SHORTHAND MANUAL has been completed.

An alternative plan which will be used by some teachers is to employ the shorthand plates of SPEED STUDIES beginning with Study VII and postpone assigning the introductory studies of each lesson until the GREGG SHORTHAND MANUAL has been completed.

Advanced Work. Attention of teachers is directed particularly to the material for reading and dictation beginning with Study XXI. This section of the book is intended to be introduced with the advanced work in business schools, and in the third semester in high schools. By dividing the reading and dictation material and vocabulary into convenient assignments, Studies XXI–XXX may be completed in one semester, leaving the last semester of high school free for the more advanced work of new dictation, transcribing and office training.

Divisions of Material in Studies. Each lesson is composed of, first, a "study" of material vital in the acquirement of speed and accuracy; second, shorthand plates (beginning with Study VII) for reading and dictation practice; third, vocabulary drills at the bottom of the shorthand pages.

Method of Handling the Studies. The work on the introductory part of each "study" should be assigned and handled exactly as a textbook lesson should be, emphasis being placed upon practical drills in writing.

Method of Handling Shorthand Plates. These should be assigned for practice in reading, and a sufficient number of copies required to insure familarity with the forms; after which dictation should be given until facility in writing is secured.

Method of Handling Vocabulary. After the shorthand plate has been read, the vocabulary words given at the bottom of each page should be assigned for practice until the forms are mastered. The preparation of the vocabulary should, of course, precede the dictation.

CHARLES L. SWEM

PERSONAL STENOGRAPHER AND OFFICIAL REPORTER TO PRESIDENT WILSON. STUDY THE WRITING POSITION MR. SWEM ASSUMES AT THE DESK

by the student himself — and that is his own study and application. The words of Emerson, "Thou shalt be paid exactly for what thou hast done, no more, no less," apply with striking force to the study of shorthand. The student will get out of shorthand just what he puts into it — no more, no less. And what he gets out of it will depend very largely upon his attitude of mind.

If he approaches the subject with enthusiasm for it, with the aim in view of perfecting himself in it for the sheer joy of achievement, without thought of the ultimate results, his success is assured. Some of the most prominent men and women in commercial and professional life to-day got their start in the world through the opportunities that shorthand offered. But they were invariably good stenographers *first.* They threw their whole energy into becoming experts in the profession they had selected, and the habit formed of doing things well extended to all their other activities. The result was that when the big opportunities came they were ready for them. Their skill in shorthand and typewriting had attracted the attention of those higher up, and they were given opportunities that were denied those of lesser skill.

Correct Habits Vital. — The late Professor James, the great psychologist of Harvard University, brings out the power of habit most graphically in his book on psychology. He lays down some maxims that should be embedded deeply into the consciousness of every student of stenography. "Could the young but realize how soon they will become mere walking bundles of habits," says Professor James, "they would give more heed to their conduct while in the plastic state. We are spinning our fates, good or evil, never to be undone."

All habits, good or bad, are the heritage of youth.

Study the Easy Position of Mr. Swem's Hand — The Hand that Wrote 268 Words a Minute for Five Minutes in the National Shorthand Reporters' Speed Contest

"The great thing in all education," he continues, "is to make our nervous system our ally instead of our enemy. We must make automatic and habitual as many useful actions as we can, and guard against growing into ways that are likely to be a disadvantage to us. The more the details of our daily life we can shorten owing to the effortless custody of automatism, the more our higher powers of mind will be set free for their own proper work."

He lays down four principles that are vitally important:

"First: In the acquisition of a new habit, or the leaving-off of an old one, we must take care to launch ourselves with as strong and decided an *initiative* as possible.

"Second: Never suffer an *exception* to occur till the new habit is rooted in your life.

"Third: Seize the very first possible opportunity to act on every resolution you make and on every emotional prompting you may experience in the direction of habits you aspire to gain."

Shorthand is a habit-forming study. Each step in your work, therefore, should be considered very carefully so that correct habits may be acquired at the start, for it is next to impossible to overcome habits that have once become fixed—transferred to the automatic process. The object to be sought in studying the art of shorthand writing is to build up a set of automatic actions as quickly and as thoroughly as possible. Every detail leading to this end must be studied and practiced. There is hardly any other practical art in which the study of economical habits of movement and of efficiency methods yields such large returns as in the technique of shorthand writing. Such mechanical details as the kind of materials you use—pen, pencil, notebook, etc.—become of very great importance.

But of greater importance still are the personal habits you acquire of thought, of posture, of execution, etc.

Materials. — The good workman invariably demands good tools. He knows that the best work is only possible when the material necessities are of high quality. Careful attention should, therefore, be given to the materials with which you work.

Notebooks. — The notebook especially is of importance. The surface of the paper should be firm and smooth in order to enable you to employ a light touch — the lighter the better. It should be free from imperfections in texture. The size most generally recommended by the best writers is six by nine inches. The lines preferably should be one-third of an inch apart, as this spacing of the lines will tend to develop a more compact style of writing. The page should have a vertical ruling down the middle so as to afford two columns for writing on each page. A column three inches wide enables you to write correctly across the line of writing without shifting the arm to any appreciable degree. If a pencil is used a slightly rougher surface is necessary.

Pen or Pencil. — Whether the pen or pencil is the better instrument for shorthand writing is a much discussed question, but the consensus of opinion of the most experienced and fastest writers is that the pen is to be preferred. The pen gives a firm, distinct outline that is easily recognized. The small circles and hooks especially can be much more readily and accurately executed with the pen than with the pencil. Pen-writing is also very much easier to read because it is generally more accurate. The more distinct lines of pen-writing make the reading far easier on the eyes.

A pen should be selected which has a fairly fine, but smooth, point. The kind of point best adapted to the hand can only be ascertained by a little experiment. While many writers prefer the ordinary dip pen, the fountain pen has so many advantages that it is to be recommended in all cases.

If a pencil is used — and many writers prefer it in spite of its known disadvantages — the student should be supplied with a sufficient number of well-sharpened pencils to obviate the necessity of writing with a dull point. A dull point influences the writing in a very marked degree. Pencil notes are apt to be large and inaccurately formed, and as the pencil dulls this tendency grows, making the notes very difficult to read.

Posture. — Perhaps no other feature of shorthand writing contributes so much to the ease, speed and accuracy of writing as does the position the writer assumes at the table. In the teaching of penmanship great emphasis is laid upon the correct posture. Posture becomes of even greater importance in shorthand writing, for shorthand not only must be written correctly, but to become highly useful it must be *written at a very rapid rate of speed.* The shorthand writer is also often required to write at a high rate of speed for long periods of time. Sustained effort thus becomes a necessity. Since each character he writes in shorthand is fraught with greater meaning, it must be executed with much greater care even at the higher speeds.

The position at the desk should receive the most earnest attention of all writers who wish to become rapid and skillful. In order that the student may gain an accurate idea of the best posture, illustrations of the position of some of the best writers of the system are presented. An analysis of these illustrations, and a study of the technique of the best writers, will show that

FREDERICK H. GURTLER

THE WRITING POSITION OF MR. FREDERICK H. GURTLER, COURT AND CONVENTION REPORTER, EX-VICE-PRESIDENT OF THE NATIONAL SHORTHAND REPORTERS' ASSOCIATION, AND WINNER OF THE FAMOUS MINER MEDAL

the majority of writers sit squarely in front of the desk with both forearms resting on it. The notebook or paper is placed in a line with the right forearm so that the hand can be moved across the line of writing without shifting the arm. The body is bent, it will be noticed, from the hips. In no case does the writer "slump" over his work with the shoulders pressed forward, but the chest is wide open to permit of free breathing. The writer should sit far enough away so that the edge of the table does not press against his body. The feet should be planted firmly on the floor. Many beginners twist their feet around the legs of the chair and assume all sorts of awkward and erratic positions very much to the detriment of their progress.

Illustration of Correct Position for Note-taking While Standing. Posed by George S. McClure

When the body is bent slightly forward a little weight will be resting on the elbows and forearms. The back should be perfectly straight from the hips to the shoulders. The weight of the arm is carried by the heavy muscles of the forearm, and the movements of the hand, wrist and fingers can be executed with the minimum of effort. It does not follow that a comfortable position is a correct one. Through habit you may have accustomed yourself to a very awkward position. To find out whether you are assuming an incorrect position ask your teacher to watch you closely during the time you are taking notes and to offer suggestions.

Position of Hand and Arm. — The position of the right hand and arm is of just as great importance as is that of the body.

Illustrations on page 10 show two views of the correct position of hand and forearm. Study particularly the slant of the pen, the position of fingers, and the method of grasping the pen. The hand and arm must have the maximum of flexibility and freedom. Since the best writers of shorthand make use of the muscular movement, and this method has everything in its favor, it should be cultivated from the very beginning of the study of the art.

The large muscles of the arm are much more capable of

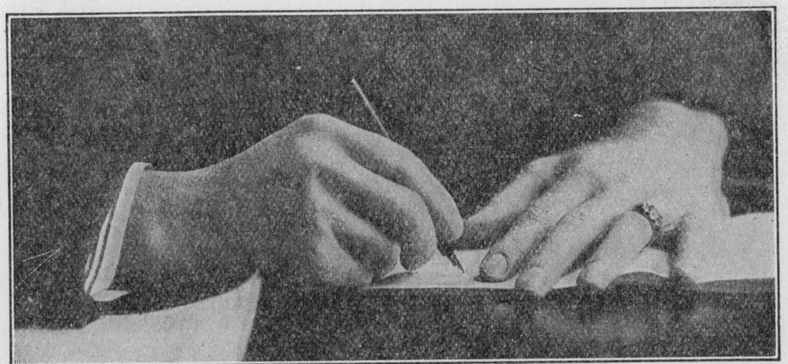

ILLUSTRATION OF PROPER METHOD OF HOLDING NOTEBOOK FLAT. POSED BY MR. GURTLER

sustained effort than are the muscles of the fingers; but unfortunately they cannot be trained to as high a degree of nicety of movement as can those of the fingers. A study of the writing movements of the most rapid writers shows that both finger and wrist movements are used. The best results can be obtained when a judicious blending of these movements is employed. As an illustration: such characters as *p*, *b*, *f*, *v*, can be executed much more readily and quickly if the downward sweep is a combination of arm and finger movement. The circles and hooks can also be executed with greater speed if the finger movement is combined with arm and wrist movement.

Keep the wrist and ball of the hand from touching the paper or the desk, but the whole forearm from the elbow to the wrist should rest on the table. With the second, third and fourth fingers turned in, as shown in the illustrations, the hand will be in a position to glide easily on the nails of these fingers.

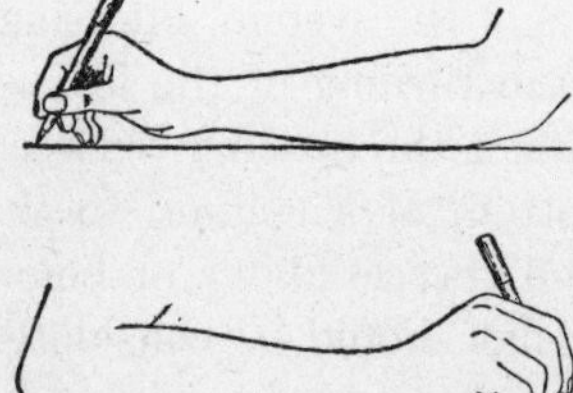

Illustration of Correct Position of Hand and Arm

Hold the pen with just enough pressure to give you command of it, but do not grip it so firmly and tenaciously that all flexibility of movement is destroyed. Gripping the pen with a death-like hold is one of the most common habits young and inexperienced writers acquire, and it is fatal to high speed and to ease of execution.

In all arts "form" or "technique" is of vast importance. Study the work of the violinist, the pianist, the golfer, the tennis player, and it will be seen that the experts have acquired a certain grace of form, an art in execution that at once appeals to us because of its obvious effectiveness.

The late David Wolfe Brown, the famous congressional reporter, says: "Pen gripping, involving as it does needless muscular effort, tends to promote an inartistic style of writing, interferes with the acquisition of speed, and induces undue and premature fatigue, to say nothing of the ultimate danger of pen paralysis from the unnecessary, excessive and long-continued muscular strain."

Light Touch. — A light touch of pen or pencil upon the paper is necessary to high speed. Using a heavy touch means gripping the pen; it destroys all flexibility of movement and it also retards speed and leads to inaccuracy. No more pressure should be exerted than is necessary to make a clear, definite outline.

Efficiency Methods. — Much of the speed displayed by the fastest writers of shorthand is acquired by a study and practice of efficiency methods in performing their work. The elimination of waste mechanical motion has almost as much to do with speed in writing as does the shortening of outlines or the application of the abbreviating principles of the system, phrasing, etc. The position of the notebook, the turning of the leaves, the passing from one outline to another, the spacing between the outlines, the passing from the bottom of a column to the top of the next, the distance the hand travels above or below the line of writing — all are factors that should be considered very carefully and analyzed by the student who wishes to acquire high speed as well as accuracy. The proper time to make a study of these features of the writing *is at the start, before incorrect habits are formed.*

Turning the Leaves of the Notebook. — To the inexperienced writer the turning of a leaf of his notebook is always attended with a sense of hurry and fear that something will be lost, especially if the dictation is pushing him to the limit of his speed. A little study and practice will enable the writer to turn the leaves without appreciable loss of time.

The following description of the proper method of turning the leaves is the result of much study and practice on the part of the talented reporter, Thomas Allen Reed. He says: "While writing on the upper half of the leaf introduce the second finger of the left hand between it and the next leaf, keeping the leaf just being written on steady by the first finger

SALOME LANNING TARR

Getting a Leaf in Position for Easy Turning is Illustrated by Miss Tarr, Who Established the World's Record for Accuracy in the Fifth International Shorthand Speed Contest. See Page 11 for Description of Method of Turning Leaves

and thumb. While writing on the last part of the page shift the leaf by degrees until it is about halfway up the book; when it is convenient, lift the first finger and thumb and the leaf will turn by itself. This is the best plan while writing on a desk or table. When writing on the knee, the first finger should be introduced instead of the second, and the leaf be shifted up only about two inches. The finger should be introduced at the first pause the speaker makes or at any convenient opportunity that presents itself."

Mr. Isaac S. Dement, one of the most expert shorthand writers the world has ever known, preferred handling the notebook much as Mr. Reed has described, but he kept shifting constantly upward the page upon which he was writing so that when the writer finished one page he would be in a position to begin the second page without having to move the hand from the bottom of the notebook to the top of the next page.

Passing from One Outline to Another. — The writer should cultivate from the start the art of passing directly from one outline to another without any preliminary or useless movements. It is axiomatic that the shortest distance between two points is a straight line. The best time to practice this method is while taking dictation which has been practiced, as the attention can then be concentrated entirely on the movement used in passing from one word to another, and the mind not diverted by trying to recall unfamiliar outlines or in constructing new ones.

By observing the work of poorly trained writers it will be seen that the pen makes several unnecessary movements at the completion of each wordform — the writer seemingly trying to get a running start by making several movements in the air. These movements result in a loss of valuable nervous energy. They are generally the result of the hesitation caused by trying to recall principles or wordsigns of which the writer has but a hazy recollection.

By memorizing a short passage and writing it repeatedly from memory, passing *directly from one outline to the next,* much may be done to overcome this very wasteful habit. The idea to be held in mind constantly is continuity of movement. In acquiring this movement a certain deliberation must at first be observed; the desire to keep the hand moving, except in performing the actual act of writing outlines, should be repressed.

In passing from one outline to another do not raise the pen higher from the paper than is necessary to clear it, for it must be remembered that the farther the pen travels the longer it takes, and unnecessary travel records itself in decreased efficiency.

From the first, aim to acquire an easy, rapid — but accurate — formation of the characters and to make each character with a *continuous* movement. Continuous does not necessarily imply *rapid.* One good way to acquire this is to make a mental picture of the entire shorthand form of a word or phrase before writing it. If you are about to write the word "make," for example, think of the consonants "m" and "k" and where the vowel should go — outside the angle — and then write the entire word with an easy, flowing movement. If you cannot write the wordform without a jerky movement the first time you attempt it, keep on writing it until you can. That is one of the very greatest of the "speed secrets." Acquire the habit early and it will help you immensely all through the Studies and enable you to acquire a higher degree of skill than you possibly could in any other way. The same principle applies to phrasing.

Spacing Between Outlines. — The spacing between outlines should be no more than is necessary to give a proper clearance between outlines. It should be uniform as far as possible.

Size of Notes. — Adopt a size of notes that seems natural to you. The characters given in this text and in the Gregg Writer are a good size to follow as a standard. As a general thing, students make characters too large, and, as this tendency is magnified in rapid writing, much is to be gained by starting with notes that are rather small. The size of notes, however, is a point that must be determined largely by the writer himself, but he should consult with his teacher and aim to adopt a size which facilitates execution. The size should be such as to give a natural freedom of movement, but this should be determined only after earnest analysis.

Correcting Outlines. — While practicing for speed and accuracy, or taking dictation, the writer should never under any circumstances *correct or change wordforms while writing*. Making incorrect outlines is mostly a matter of habit. It is just as easy to acquire the habit of writing correctly as it is to write incorrectly. The loss of time in crossing out words incorrectly written is equivalent to that of writing several words correctly, to say nothing of the mental disturbance it causes. The time to make corrections in outlines is *while reading or transcribing the notes*. Then every poorly executed outline should receive careful attention and sufficient practice obtained in writing the *correct form* to establish ease of execution.

Concentrating the Attention. — Facility in writing reaches the highest point only when the writer can give his undivided attention to the work in hand. The writer should never let

PAULA E. WERNING

THE WRITING POSITION OF MISS PAULA E. WERNING, HOLDER OF THE FIRST CERTIFIED SHORTHAND REPORTER CERTIFICATE ISSUED IN NEW YORK STATE. SPEED RECORD, 232 WORDS A MINUTE ON JURY CHARGE IN NATIONAL SHORTHAND REPORTERS' CONTEST

his attention be diverted if he can possibly avoid it. He should even accustom himself to continue his writing when the most startling causes for interruption appear. Holding command of the attention is an art that cannot be too strongly emphasized.

Systematic Methods of Arranging the Notebook. — By following a systematic method the notebook of the stenographer can be arranged so that any letter or any piece of dictation can be referred to quickly. At the beginning of each day's work the notebook should be dated. The beginning of each dictation or letter should be indicated by some landmark. If the dictation consists of letters the name of each firm should begin on a new line and be indented. Form the habit of writing names in shorthand. The vast majority of names can be written just as accurately in shorthand as in longhand. It is only the name of unusual spelling that needs to be written in longhand.

As each piece of dictation is transcribed, draw a vertical line down through it to indicate that the matter has been transcribed or read. In reading, circle each outline that has been imperfectly executed and afterwards practice the correct form for each of these encircled wordforms as has been suggested in the foregoing. A rubber band should be slipped over the leaves of the notebook preceding the beginning of a day's work, so that the place of writing can be quickly found when it is desired to refer to any of the early dictation of the day.

General Principles To Be Applied

To become expert in writing and in reading shorthand, these principles should be kept in mind:

First, that the principles of the system must be applied ac-

JOSEPH M. SHAFFER

Writing Position of Mr. Joseph M. Shaffer, Who Holds the World's Record for Accuracy at 175 Words a Minute on Solid Matter, Making but One Error (Due to Mishearing) in Five Minutes' Dictation—99.99% Perfect

curately and intelligently in order to give the required brevity of form and to produce uniformity in writing.

Second, that the proportion of the characters must be constantly observed. That is, a careful distinction must be made in the length of strokes and in the size of circles.

Third, much practice must be obtained in applying principles and in the execution of the characters in order to secure facility.

Fourth, everything written must be read — even the forms made in practicing the simple characters of the alphabet. The shorthand characters should be analyzed, criticized and studied until an accurate style of writing has become a habit.

Fifth, frequent and thorough reviews are essential to rapid and sure progress. The review should not be confined solely to "mental" review, but should be accompanied by much practice in writing. A deep impression of the principles can be acquired only by such reviews intelligently conducted. Each time the writer goes over a principle thoughtfully with the mind concentrated on it, the deeper will become the impression of that principle.

Sixth, shorthand is a habit-forming study; habits are acquired not by doing a thing once but by repetition.

Seventh, as much as possible of actual writing should be done from dictation, or from copying well-written shorthand. Copying from printed matter is useful, but since shorthand writing is nearly always done from dictation it is evident that practice of this kind is preferable. The student, however, should form the habit of writing all of his original compositions and notes in shorthand. We learn shorthand by *using* it.

SPEED STUDY I

FIRST LESSON

Speed and accuracy in shorthand writing begin with the very first lesson. They depend almost wholly upon two things: first, the clearness of the mental picture of each form the student has in mind; and, second, upon his ability to execute correctly and with rapidity the movements which are necessary to reproduce the picture. A good shorthand style depends eventually, not upon what the writer has in mind, but upon what he can put on paper. It means clear vision plus *mastery of movement.*

An analysis of Gregg Shorthand shows that there are certain elementary combinations which are repeated, with slight variations, over and over again — even in the most advanced writing. A mastery of these movements, it is obvious, will therefore give the writer a firm foundation upon which to build his structure of speed and accuracy.

In studying the drills, aim first at securing a *clear mental picture* of the form to be executed; analyze carefully the movement necessary to make it rapidly, and then repeat the movement until facility is acquired. At the beginning a careful comparison of the notes written with the correct forms in the text is essential. The comparison should be carried on until the habit of correct movement has been established. The characters are to be *written*, not drawn. Two important features to be looked after constantly are: first, length of consonant strokes; and, second, sizes of circles and hook vowels.

Consonants. — In practicing the following drill, make a positive distinction in the length of strokes:

Drill 1

Consonant Combinations. — The joining of curves, and especially unequal curves is a point that needs emphasis.

Drill 2

Equal Curves		*Unequal Curves*	
kr		kl	
gl		rg	
rk		gr	
lg		lk	

Circle Vowels. — In writing the circle vowels, sizes must be carefully distinguished. It is important to note that circles may be written in either direction — from right to left or the reverse — depending upon the nature of the joining. Practice writing in both directions.

Drill 3

o o o ₒ ₒ ₒ o o o ₒ ₒ ₒ o o o ₒ ₒ ₒ o o o ₒ ₒ ₒ

ₒ o ₒ o ₒ o ₒ o ₒ o ₒ o ₒ o ₒ o ₒ o ₒ

Circle Vowels Joined to Curves. — In joining circle vowels to curves no part of the circle should be retraced. Observe carefully the movement used in starting and finishing the circle as indicated by the dotted arrow:

Right way:

By retracing the circle, as shown in the following illustration, much time will be wasted:

Wrong way:

Practice the joining of both large and small circles at the beginning and end of each consonant. Form the habit of *completely closing the circle.*

Inside Curves. — There should be no space between the circle and the consonant.

Drill 4

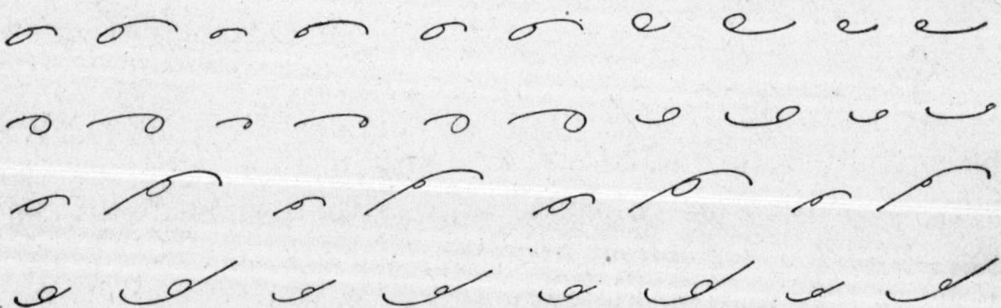

Outside Angles. — In joinings of the following type the circle cuts the line of writing: ....

Drill 5

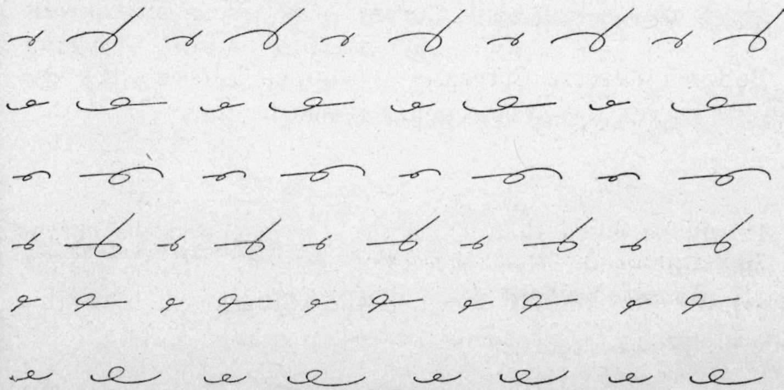

Circles Joined to Straight Strokes. — In joining the circle to straight strokes, start or finish the circle as shown by the dotted lines in the following illustration:

Right way:

Wrong way:

In the following drill join the circle with the forward movement:

Drill 6

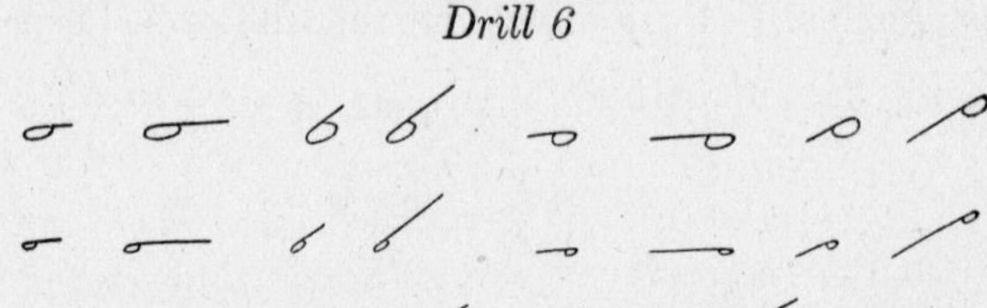

Between Reverse Curves. — When a circle occurs between reverse curves, the circle should join snugly, thus:

Right way:

It will be noted that if the circle were erased the curves would still retain their correct formation. If the joining has not been skillfully executed the outlines will have this appearance:

Wrong way:

Drill 7

Key: gale, lag, kale, lake, rig, gear, kill, gill, click, rag, leak, drag, wreck, trigger, caret, trick, league, racket, rake.

SPEED STUDY II

SECOND LESSON

Speed in the execution of the consonants presented in the Second Lesson of the Manual can be increased by combining muscular movement with a slight closing of the fingers with the downward sweep of the pen. Speed is vastly increased by eliminating all unnecessary movements. Analyze the movements necessary to execute a form. Pass from one character to another in the most direct line, with the pen barely clearing the paper. Do not stop at the end of a character.

Observe length very carefully — but *write* the characters.

Drill 1

Consonants Joined. — The combinations *pr*, *br*, *fr*, *pl*, *bl*, *fl*, are of very frequent occurrence, and special attention to the writing of them is highly essential. These frequently recurring combinations should be written with *one sweep of the pen.* Distinction in length is of vital importance.

Study very carefully the following types of joinings — the dotted lines indicate slant:

Frequent Consonant Combinations. — Note that in *pr*, *pl*, the first movement is from right to left; in *br*, *bl*, the first movement is downward.

Drill 2

Key to second and third lines: pray, bray, play, blame, apple, prate, brain, plain, bred, preach, pledge, blade, brim.

The "Fr" Blend. — The *fr*, *fl*, and *vr*, *vl* combinations — or blends — should also be executed with one movement. Study particularly the slant of *f* and *v* as indicated by the dotted lines:

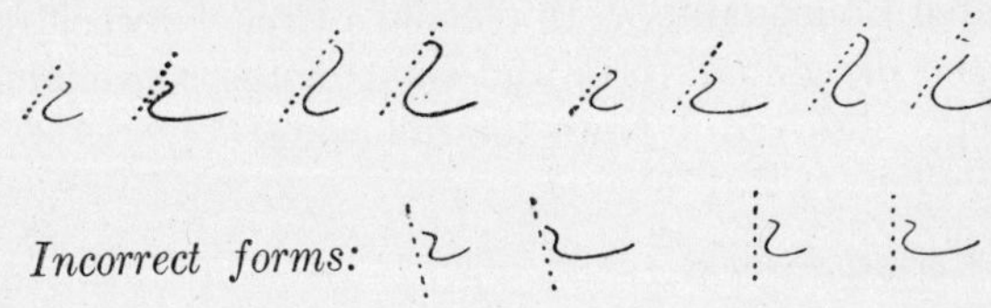

Intervening Vowels. — When a circle vowel intervenes between the *f* or *v* and a following *r* or *l*, and in other similar joinings, the angle is restored and the circle placed outside, thus:

Key: fear, feel, fair, fail, vary, valley.

In harmony with the *fr* and *fl* blends, such combinations as the following should receive study and practice:

Key: keep, can-be.

Practice the following words, which form a nucleus for other combinations of this character, until facility in writing the *fr* and *fl* blends is acquired:

Drill 3

Key: free, fray, frame, flay, flame, flat, freed, fresh, flee, frail, flit, flash, flail, flag, French.

Repeated Consonants.—In placing a circle between repeated strokes the distinctive form and slant of the consonants must be properly observed. Note the following:

Correct Forms:

By comparing the following incorrect forms with the foregoing the importance of correct slant will be evident:

Incorrect forms:

Note the *different* slants, as indicated by the dotted lines.

Facile Joinings.—In the following joinings, observe how each consonant stands out distinctly, and how both slant and economy of effort in joining are fully preserved:

Drill 4

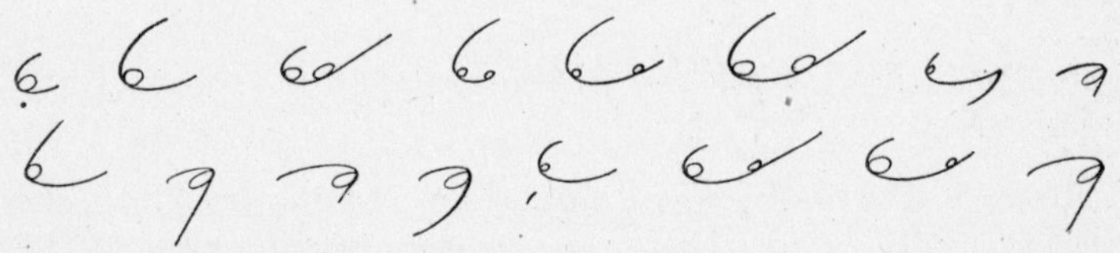

Key: par, bail, parade, berry, billet, ballad, shelf, cash, jail, cage, gash, cave, peel, pallid, pallet, gage.

In such joinings as *p-a-r*, for example, the circle should close up snugly.

In such combinations as the following a very full curve produces a more facile joining:

Drill 5

Key: deep, evade, fish, batch, calm, latch, peach, chap, chief, knave.

Straight Strokes.—Attention must also be given to the execution of straight lines. Because of the apparent simplicity, the execution of the straight stokes is often neglected. Better outlines will be made automatically if the methods of joining the circle explained on page 23 of the preceding Study are observed. Note particularly in the following that the straight characters are really straight and that the curves are distinct:

Drill 6

Key: each, hatch, edge, age, she, jay, if, after, every, I-have, pay, believe.

Reverse Curves. — There are a few words in which the reverse curves in this lesson are found in combination. The following illustrations should be practiced carefully:

Drill 7

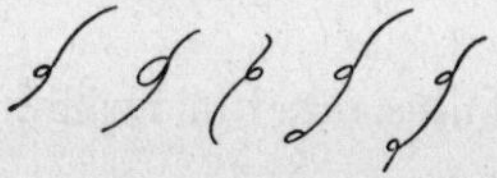

Key: beef, pave, fib, bevy, peevish.

Modification of Circles. — The mastery of the joinings illustrated in paragraphs fifteen and sixteen of the Manual is of very great importance.

Drill 8

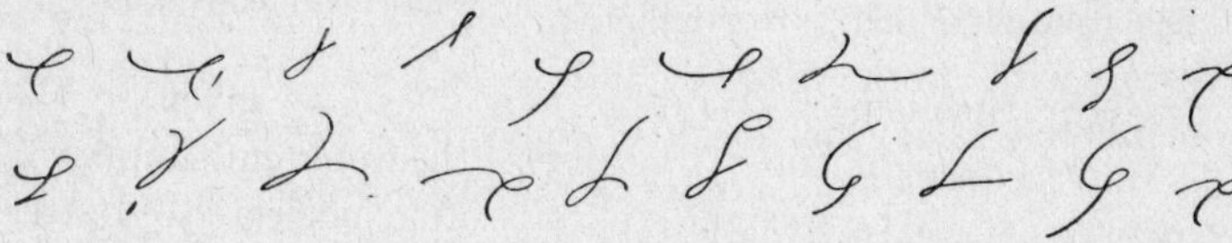

Key: rap, leap, chat, dish, rave, lash, fickle, bit, taffy, cab, raft, fade, vague, gap, back, abate, brief, beam, brave, cap.

SPEED STUDY III

THIRD LESSON

O-hook. — The O-hook should be made small, narrow, and deep. It should have the proper slant also, and should be written so that the start and finish of the hook are parallel with the line of writing. Illustration:

Drill 1

Observe the comparative sizes of the three characters of this group—*o, r, l*—as illustrated in Drill 2.

Drill 2

O-hook Joined. — The joining of the O-hook to other characters is a point in the technique of writing that should receive close attention. Observe carefully the combinations in the following drill, after which practice each until it can be written with both facility and accuracy. It should be remembered that the object of these drills is to secure accuracy and speed in *movement*, and the drills should be practiced until the correct movement is a matter of habit. The drill will give facility in joining the O-hook initially and finally to all consonants.

Drill 3

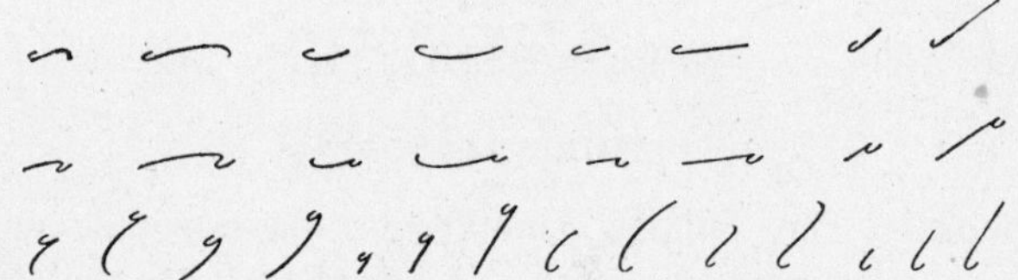

In the majority of cases the O-hook joins naturally without an angle. In joining the O-hook after *k* and *g* the movement is similar to that in writing *gr* — there should be no stop.

Drill 4

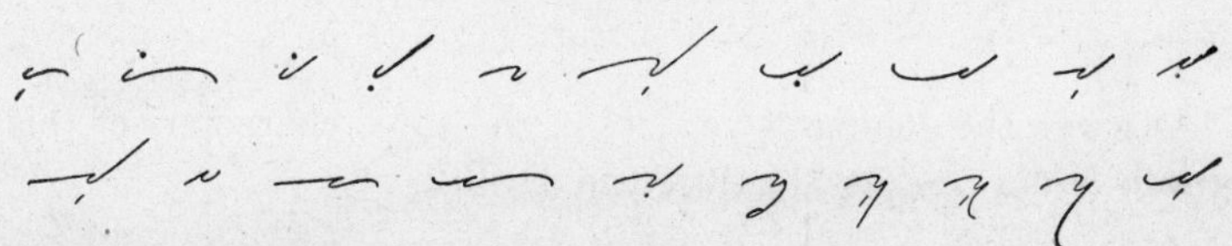

Key: oak, hog, hot, awed, call, goad, wrought, lot, note, taught, mode, told, mock, rogue, caught, coffee, coach, cope, cob, wrote.

O-hook to Down Strokes. — It will be seen that the O-hook joins without an angle after the downward characters. The following words will furnish drill in executing this joining:

Drill 5

Key: pole, bawl, fawn, volley, shawl, chore, jolly, polo, bore, Jove, bone, bob, shore, shop, pope, bowl, fop, chopper, job.

O-hook Blend. — Between *f, v, p, b* and a following *k* or *g*, the O-hook is indicated by rounding the angle, thus:

Drill 6

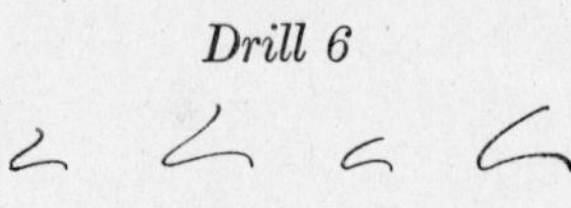

Key: folk, vogue, poke, bog

O-hook on Side. — The following words will furnish drill in turning the O-hook on its side before *n, m, r, l:*

Drill 7

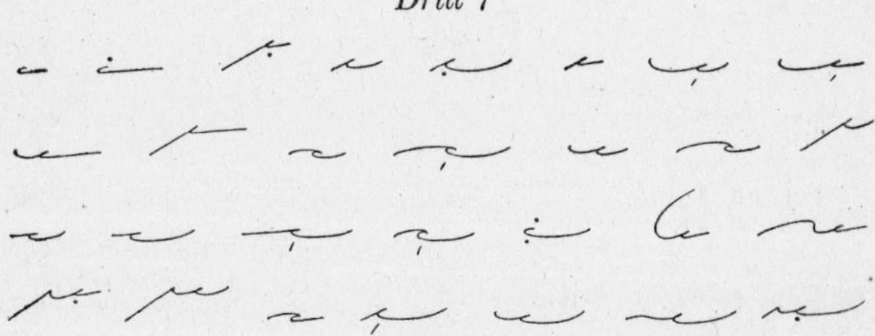

Key: on, home, dawn, tore, tall, tone, lower, loan, roam, dome, core, goal, roar, gore, door, nor, knoll, mole, coal, hall, brawn, grown, drawn, drawer, cone, toll, roll, crawl, trawl.

SPEED STUDY IV

FOURTH LESSON

OO-hook. — The observations made on page 30 with regard to the formation of the O-hook apply with equal accuracy to the OO-hook. Study the following illustration:

Drill 1

Study the comparative sizes of the three characters of this group, *oo*, *k*, *g*.

Drill 2

OO-hook Joined. — The following drill will furnish practice in the joining of the OO-hook initially and finally to all consonants:

Drill 3

As is the case with the O-hook, the OO-hook joins naturally to the majority of the consonants.

Before "R" or "L."—In joining the OO-hook before *r* or *l*, the movement is similar to that used in writing *kl*—there should be no stop at the joining. Study these examples: 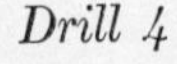

OO-hook Blend.—When *r* or *l* is followed by *p* or *b*, the hook is shown by rounding the angle, thus:

Drill 4

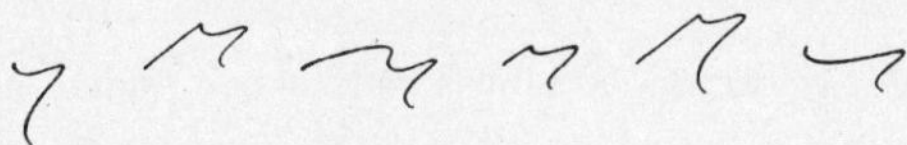

Key: rub, droop, group, troop, drub, loop.

The following words and phrases will illustrate and furnish practice in executing important types of joining:

Drill 5

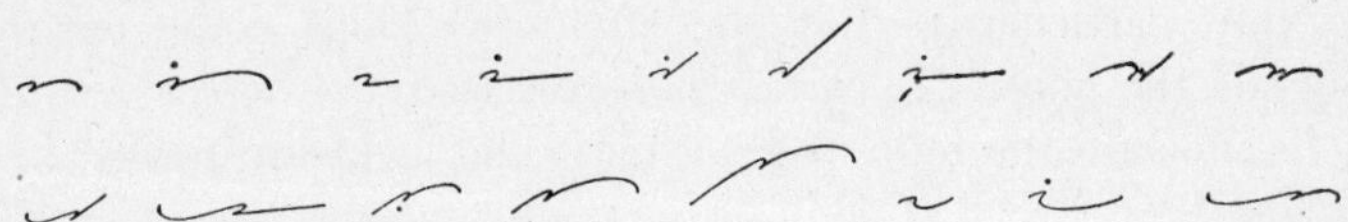

Key: you-can, hug, won, hum, hut, you-would, whom, cut, cook, rut, loom, took, tug, dug, you-are, hull, luck.

OO-hook on Side.—Turning the OO-hook on its side forms an important study in execution.

Drill 6

Key: noon, nook, null, mud, muff, coolie, gull.

OO-hook to Down Strokes. — The OO-hook preceding or following a downward stroke is a frequently recurring type of joining.

Drill 7

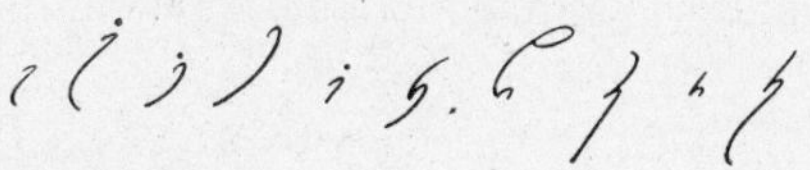

Key: up, hub, hoof, you-have, hush, puff, above, fudge, shoe, chub.

OO-hook to Circles.—When a circle or loop follows a hook it should not interfere with the characteristic form of the hook.

Correct forms:

Note particularly that the circles or loops come entirely outside the hook. If care is not exercised the hooks may degenerate into the following inartistic and awkward forms:

Incorrect forms:

Drill 8

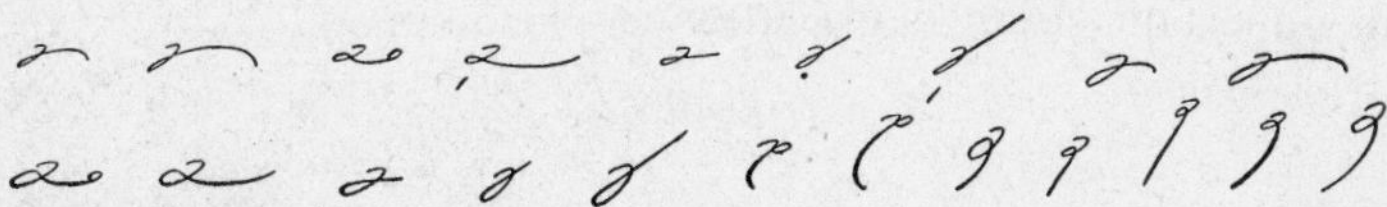

Key: wick, wig, weary, weal, win, wet, weed, wake, wag, wary, wail, wane, wait, wade, weep, web, waif, witch, wedge, weave, wave.

Hooks Joined. — Observe how consecutive hooks are joined.

Drill 9

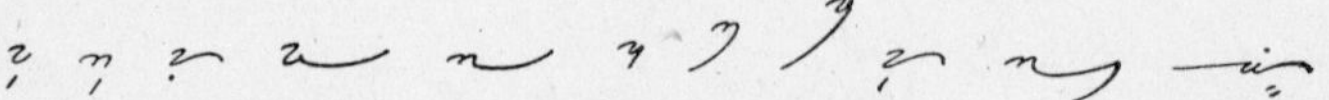

Key: woe, woo, walk, wall, wool, wash, woof, wove, woke, wolf, Mohawk.

Dash for "W." — When the dash is used to express *w* within a word, skill is necessary to insert the dash with precision.

Drill 10

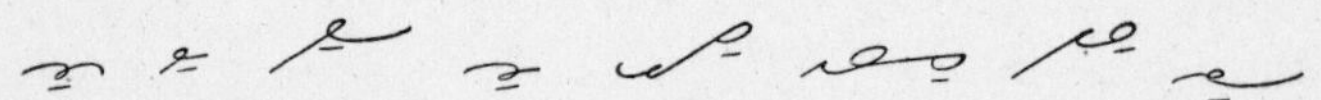

Key: quick, twin, dwell, queen, roadway, tramway, doorway, quill.

"Wh" Combination. — In *wh* the dot for *h* is invariably made first.

Drill 11

Key: whit, whack, whim, wheel, Whig, whiff, wheat, whip, whale, whinny.

"Ye" and "Ya' Loops. — The distinction in the infrequent movements used in the execution of the *ye* and *ya* loops, as distinguished from joined circles, should be carefully analyzed and practiced.

Drill 12

Key: yam, yak, year, yell, Yale, yet, yelp, yegg.

SPEED STUDY V

FIFTH LESSON

The Joining of "S."—The *s* sound is one of the most frequent in the English language. Mastery of the joining of this character is therefore very important.

The following drill is intended to develop skill in making a distinction in length between *s* and *p*, *b*; between *s* and *f*, *v*:

Drill 1

Joining "S" to Curves.—When *s* is joined to a downward curve it is important to get "around the corner" quickly; *uniform slant* should be maintained. Give particular attention to the joining of *s* before *r*, *l*, and after *k*, *g*, thus:

Drill 2

Joining "S" to Straight Lines.—*S* joins to straight lines with a sharp angle, but there should be no pause at the joining.

Drill 3

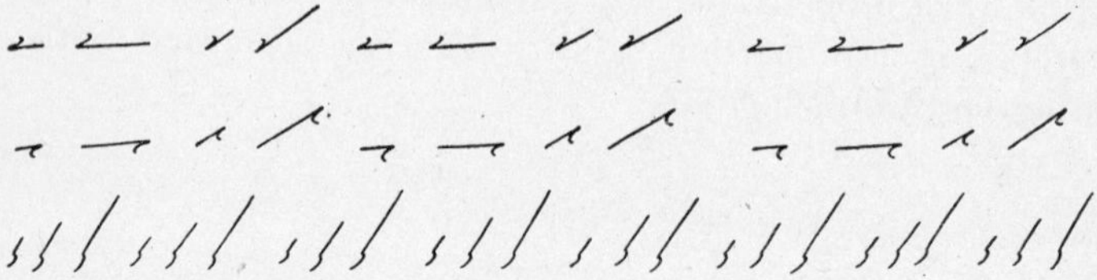

Intervening Circles. — When a circle intervenes, the form does not change.

Drill 4

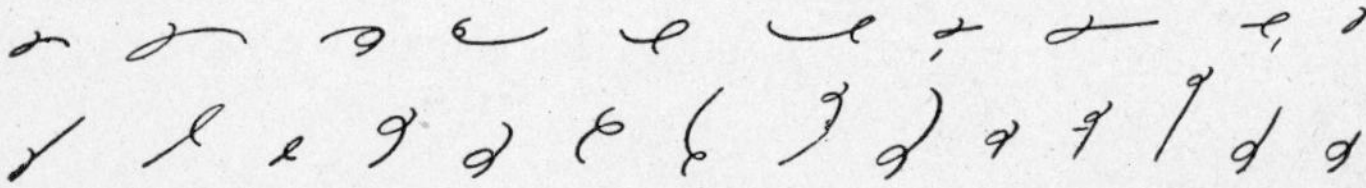

Key: sick, sag, case, seal, race, lease, scene, same, niece, seat, said, days, teas, safe, face, sap, bees, sieve, vase, sash, switch, siege, chase, chaise.

"So" and "Us." — Facility in writing the combinations *so* and *us* and other joinings of *s* to hooks can be acquired by studying and practicing the following:

Drill 5

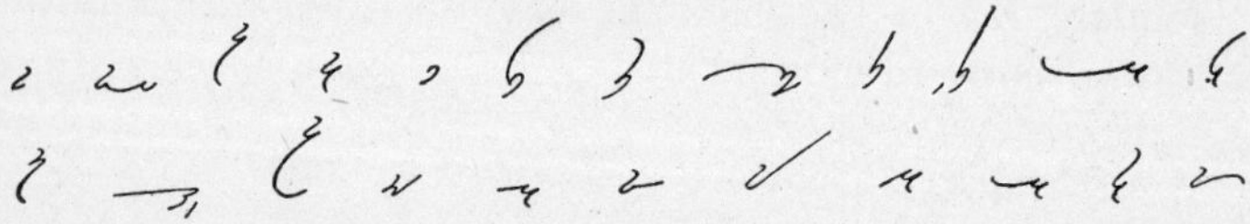

Key: so, sorrow, sop, sauce, us, bus, fuss, gust, choose, juice, laws, pause, soup, moose, sober, suit, knows, sown, sod, toes, rows, foes, soak.

The "Str" Combination. — *Str* is one of the most facile of forms when properly written. It should be executed without a stop. It is important to write *t* very *short* and with a rather vertical inclination.

Drill 6

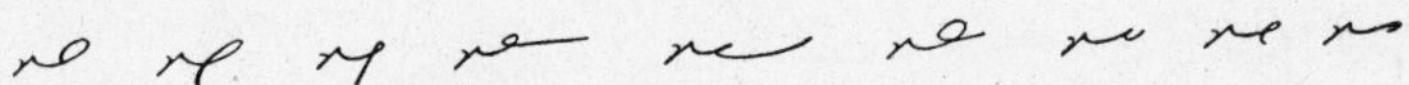

Key: stray, strap, stretch, stream, stroll, strain, straw, stress, strew.

"Th" Joined. — Practice on the following list of words and phrases will help to impress the method of joining *th*. The most frequently recurring joinings are shown.

Drill 7

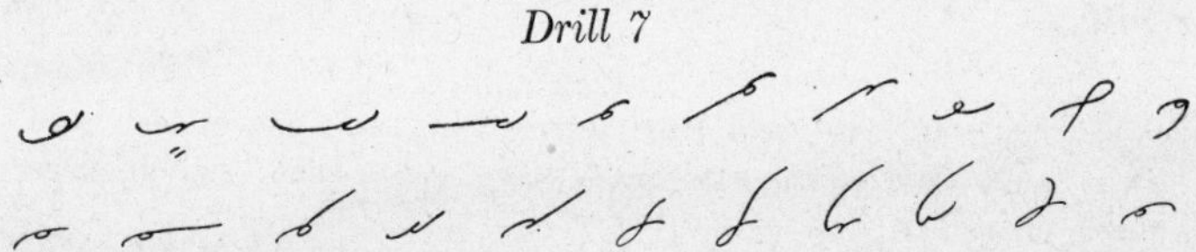

Key: wrath, Ruth, loath, moth, teeth, death, do-the, there-were, thatch, thief, thin, theme, they-would, thought, thud, path, bath, booth, both, faith, thick.

Joining "X." — The character for *x* is written with a distinct downward-forward movement.

Drill 8

Key: coax, Rex, lax, tax, vex, fox, sex, box, flax, wax, suffix, affix.

"Ng" and "Ngk." — The following forms afford sufficient practice in the execution of these characters:

Drill 9

Key: clang, clink, mink, pink, sting, tank, spring.

Suffixes "ing-thing," "ings." — The suffix *ing* should be as close to the preceding stroke as possible.

Drill 10

Key: doing, going, saying, asking, anything, something, everything, shipping, changing, risking, working, suitings, doings, trappings, moorings, sweepings, hangings, combings, innings.

Suffix "ily-ally." — The movement in writing this suffix is shown by the arrows:

Compare pretty prettily

ready readily

SPEED STUDY VI

SIXTH LESSON

The Diphthongs. — Characters for the diphthongs should be *written without a stop.* In *u, ow,* and *oi* it is important to get the circle *outside* the hook. The hook must retain its natural form.

Drill 1

The diphthongs *u, ow, oi* do not change their forms when joined. *Ow* is joined exactly in the same way as *u.* The following drill illustrates the more frequently recurring combinations. Repeat the drill substituting *ow* for *u.*

Drill 2

The following drill will give practice in executing various combinations:

Drill 3

Key: cue, cow, coy, mouth, gout, Roy, now, mew, toy, youth, bow, boy, few, fowl, void, joy, choice, yule, owl, unique.

The Diphthong "I." — An important point to be considered in executing the long *i* is that it is a *circle* and hence the rules for joining circles apply to it also.

Note particularly the joining of initial *i* to the following:

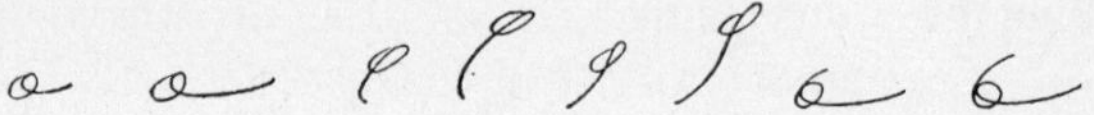

In joining *i* between characters, the character following it begins precisely where the *i* is finished. Practice the execution until the formation of *i* can be made smoothly. A common fault is that of making a pause after the indentation.

Drill 4

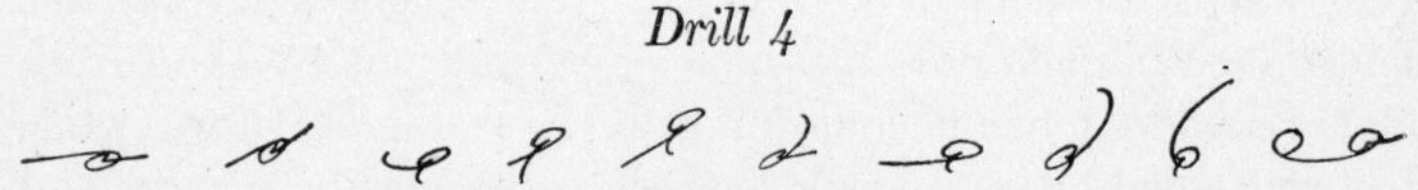

Key: mine, tight, rice, type, dice, fine, mice, vice, buys, align.

Omission of Indentation in Diphthong "I." — The following are among the most common examples:

Drill 5

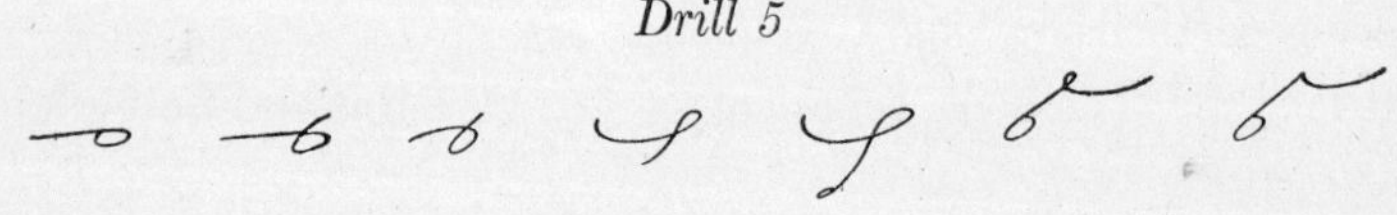

Key: my, might, quite, life, lively, ideal, idle.

Concurrent Vowel Characters. — The following drill will serve to give practice in forming these somewhat infrequent combinations:

Drill 6

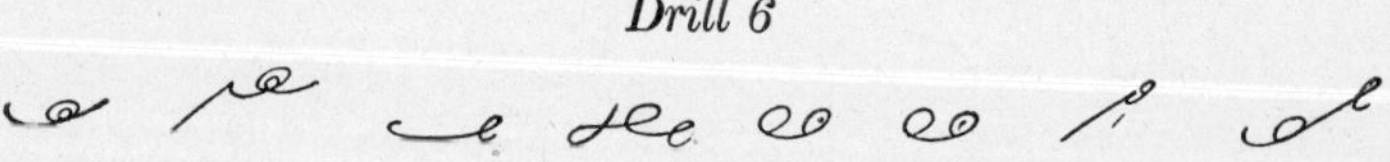

Key: riot, drier, oleo, scenario, aria, area, doughy, radio.

SPEED STUDY VII

SEVENTH LESSON

The Blended Consonants. — From the artistic viewpoint, the blended consonants form one of the most attractive features of the system. But this is merely incidental; their great practical value is the important thing.

The "Ten-den," "Tem-dem" Blends. — A very simple illustration will enable the student to learn with certainty the direction each form takes. Simply take note of the primary characters from which the blend is developed. The *length of the curve* is determined in each case by the *n* or *m*, and not by the *t* or *d*. Thus, a curved blend containing an *n* would be short, while if it contained an *m* it would be long — because *n* is short and *m* is long.

Length and Slant. — The *ten-den* is the length of *p;* the *tem-dem* the length of *b;* the *ent-end* the length of *f;* the *emt-emd* the length of *v*. Compare and study the following, noting particularly length and slant:

P B Ten-den Tem-dem F V Ent-end Emt-emd

Study the comparative sizes in the following:

th		th	
ten-den		ent-end	
tem-dem		emt-emd	

When *ten-den* or *tem-dem* begin a word an easy, graceful, and compact form is secured by an outward curve at the beginning, thus:

Right way		*Wrong way*	
temper		temper	
tenancy		tenancy	

"Def-dev," "Gent-gend."—The *def* blend begins with *d*, hence it is written upward; the *gent-gend* begins with the sound of *j*, hence is written downward. *The first consonant in the blend determines direction.* Study the following illustrations, noting particularly the size, formation and slant:

this   def-dev   gent-gend

The blends *def-dev-tive* and *gent-gend* are often called egg-shaped characters. These blends should be narrow and should curve at the *beginning* and at the *end*, thus:

Practice the following common words which bring into use the foregoing blends:

Drill 1

Key: latent, tendency, timid, threaten, brand, trained, restive, smitten, attend, freedom, soothe, sudden, tinsel, gentle, genteel, motive, native, ripened, happened, spent, defeat, divide, deficit, attentive, defame.

The principal faults in the execution of these blends are: *making the curves too flat; failure to curve at the beginning and end, thus leaving too great a space between the starting and finishing points; improper slant.*

"Men-Mem," "Ted-Ded-Det." — The blends for *men-mem, ted-ded-det* require no special treatment; the principal thing is to observe size.

t d ted-ded-det

n m men-mem

Practice the following words containing these combinations:

Drill 2

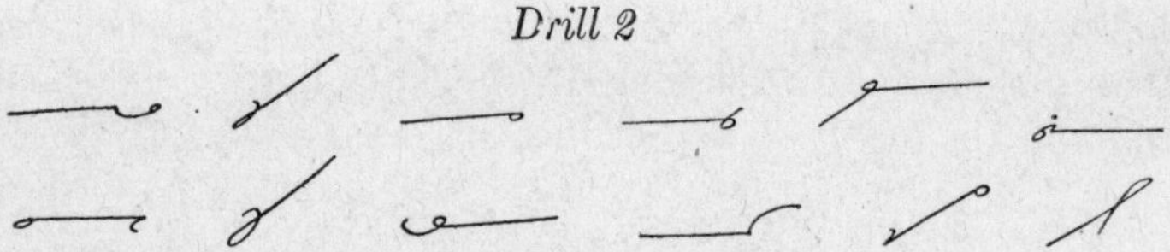

Key: memory, seated, many, minute, demon, human, immense, waited, remain, maintain, steady, detach.

The "Ses" Blends.—The *ses* blends are simply combinations of the two *s's*. These graceful, "wave-like" characters should not be given a very deep curvature. Compare:

Right way: misses pieces

Wrong way: misses pieces

In joining *ses* after a circle vowel, following or preceding another consonant, the first of the *s's* may be lost in forming part of the circle, thus:

Drill 3

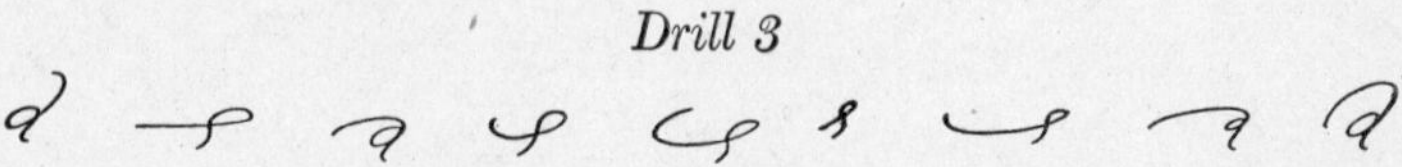

Key: faces, masses, cases, races, places, teases, leases, guesses, defaces.

When *ses* precedes or follows a consonant or hook-vowel, both *s's* are written, but with one movement. The following will show the application:

Drill 4

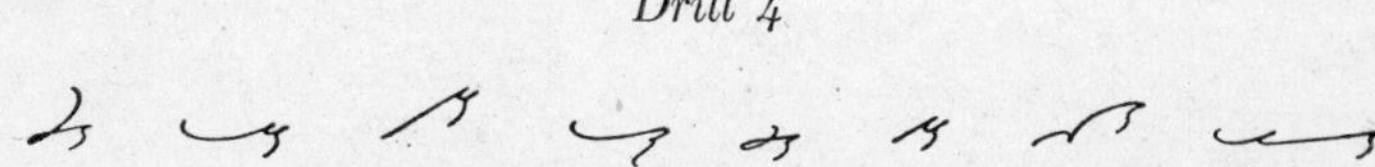

Key: fences, losses, doses, loses, senses, tosses, condenses, romances.

The combination *xs* occurs occasionally. Observe the joining.

Drill 5

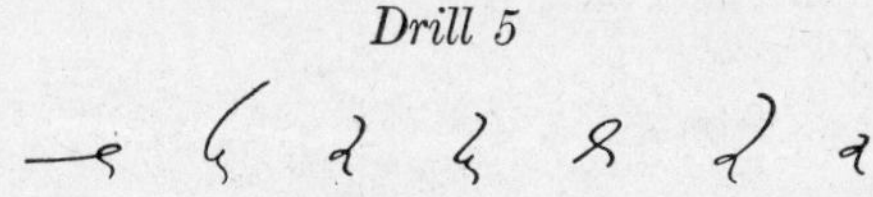

Key: mixes, boxes, fixes, foxes, taxes, vexes, sexes.

When *ted, ded,* or *ed* is indicated with a disjoined *t,* it should be written upward quite close to the preceding character.

Drill 6

Key: demanded, divided, talented, guided, printed, fainted, daunted.

BUSINESS LETTERS

1. (44)

2. (53)

3. (55)

4.

The-attention, printing, binding, classes, help, before-the, notice, monthly, I-have-your-letter, plans, season's, I-shall-be-glad, to-take, I-will-pay, does-not, appeal, at-this-time, birth, ticket, attend, sale, to-miss, we-inclose, prices, cotton, linen, suitings, you-will-need, shelves.

(73)

5.

(94)

6.

(97)

We-know, will-please, shall-we-ship, these-goods, cases, you-will-like, ready, early, and-will-be, at-that-time, if-you-wish, shop, ink, paper, every-day, you-are-saving, books, that-it-is, tennis, rackets, we-could-have, windows, sell, write-us, back, to-us, it-must-be, of-this-month.

SPEED STUDY VIII

EIGHTH LESSON

The Reversing Principle. — From the executional side, the reversing movements are quite similar to joinings already treated.

(a) In reversing the circle to express *r* on straight characters, the movement is exactly the reverse of that ordinarily employed in joining a circle to straight lines.

Compare the following forms, observing closely the direction the pen takes as indicated by the arrow, after which practice executing the movements until they can be made with facility:

To indicate *r*:

heart arm heard mere

Without *r*:

hat aim head me

The principal joinings to straight strokes are illustrated in the following drill:

Drill 1

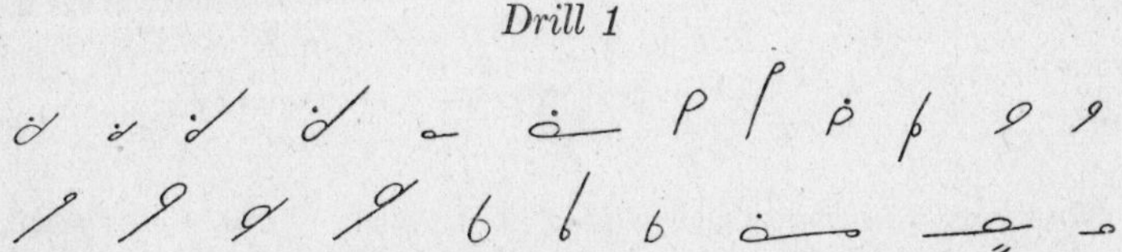

Key: heart, hurt, heard, hard, earn, harm, arch, urge, harsh, church, tare, tear, dear, dare, tart, dart, chair, jeer, share, harmony, Marne, near.

(b) In executing the forms employed in this joining, the reversing is done on the straight characters (*t, d*) or their modifications (*ten-den, tem-dem, ent-end, emt-emd*). Care should be taken to close the circle completely in each case.

Drill 2

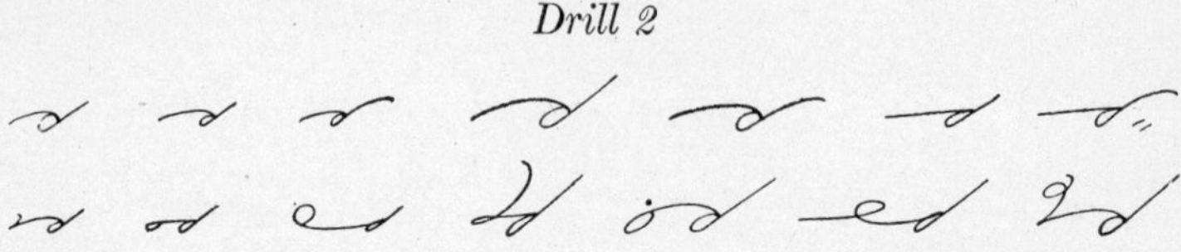

Key: cart, curt, curtain, guard, garden, mart, Martin, skirt, inert, alert, vineyard, haggard, mallard, safeguard.

(c) An important distinction is made in reversing after *p*, *b*, and in reversing after other downward characters. After *p, b*, the reversed circle is always *above* the next character; in all other joinings it is *below* the next character. The first line of the following illustration shows the method of joining after *p, b;* the second, after other downward characters:

burn barn pared barter Bert

germ charm chart farm churn

Drill 3

Key: burden, Barney, farmer, pardon, journey, chairman, Vernon, spurt, spared.

(d) The distinctive joining is also employed between *sh*, *ch*, *j*, and *l*.

Drill 4

Key: Charles, Charlie, Shirley, Charlotte, charlatan, churlish.

The movement in executing the reversed loop requires special practice.

Drill 5

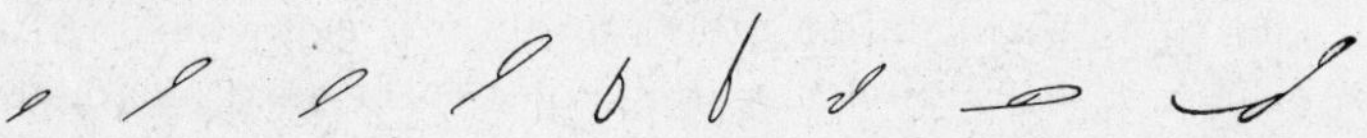

Key: tears, dears, tares, dares, shares, jeers, waters, mires, larders.

(e) The joining of the reversed circle before straight lines is similar to the joining of the reversed circle after *p*, *b*, as illustrated in (c).

Drill 6

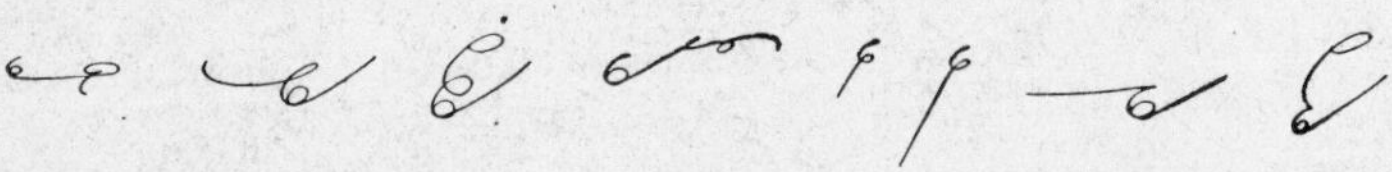

Key: surmise, lizard, haphazard, sardonic, search, surcharge, mansard, absurd.

BUSINESS LETTERS

7. (44)

8. (43)

9. (47)

10. (62)

Please-mail, chart, garden, give-me, you-wish, job, finished, we-cannot, commence, surprise, we-sent-you, trimmed, fur, serge, marten, trimmings, so-that, you-state, styles, we-are-mailing, we-believe, you-need, we-have-never, finer, as-you-desire, card, as-your-name, passed, there-will-be.

11.

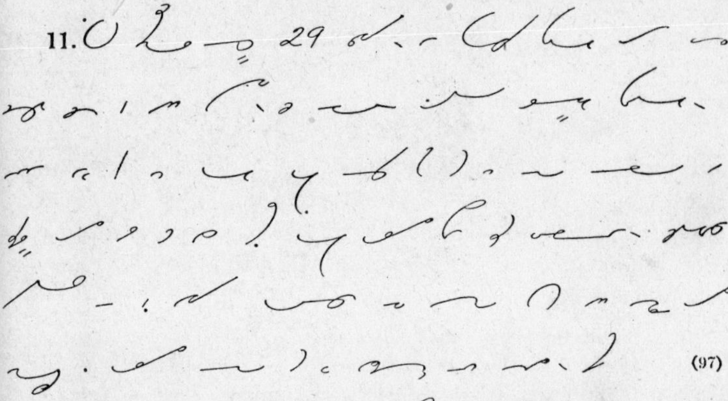

(97)

12.

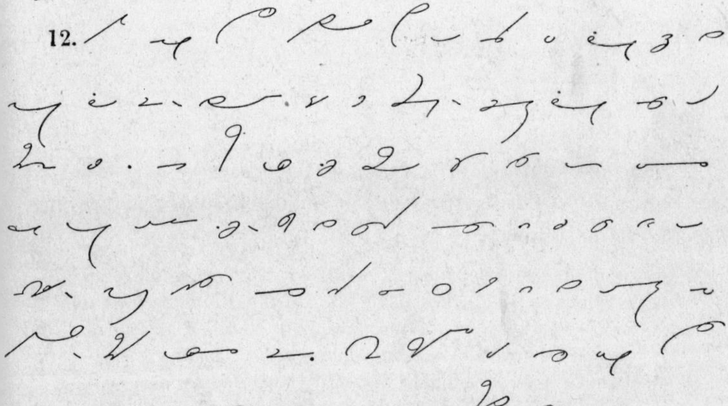

(135)

With-order, billiard, balls, no-longer, Thermos, bottles, Chester, of-next-month, we-trust-that-the, concern, you-will-find, in-your, day-letter, that-will-not, assist, very-much, we-must-have, if-you-cannot, thrown, in-this-territory, there-must-be, write-me, I-should-know, merchants, I-can-say.

SPEED STUDY IX

NINTH LESSON

Methods of Learning Wordsigns. — When we consider that more than half the words used in spoken and written language are made up of the words we know in shorthand as "wordsigns," their importance is emphasized. Mr. David Wolfe Brown, the famous Congressional reporter, says:

> "It is highly important that whatever the student undertakes to memorize should be memorized thoroughly. From half-recollection comes hesitation; and from hesitation comes loss of speed. Especially in the study of the wordsigns, most students undertake to learn too many at once. It cannot be too often repeated that in shorthand whatever needs to be memorized at all needs to be so mastered that it may come instantly to the mind and fingers whenever wanted."

As the best method of learning the wordsigns, Mr. Bernard De Bear, the well-known English reporter and teacher, has suggested the following:

> "Take a double sheet of foolscap and fold it over into folds which will give about twelve divisions in all. Copy from the textbook neatly and carefully the signs you are about to learn, one on each line. Having thus filled the first column, close the book, and endeavor at once from memory to transcribe into longhand in column two. The words having only just been copied, this should prove no difficult task; but any blanks should be filled in from the key and underlined, to denote that the signs were not remembered. This done, fold under column one, so as to leave only the longhand words in column two visible, and transcribe those into shorthand in column three, so nearly as the memory will allow. Gaps can now be filled in from column one, which, however, should not be resorted to until the attempt has been made to work through the entire list.

Then retranscribe the shorthand lines on column four. And so on to the end — shorthand into longhand, and vice versa. It may be guaranteed that by the time the twelve columns have all been filled in the manner indicated, that particular set of words or phrases will have been almost thoroughly mastered."

A point to be emphasized in learning the wordsigns is the necessity for plenty of dictation and reading practice. Because of the simplicity of most of the wordsigns, they are apt to be written more hurriedly, and consequently more carelessly, than other characters and thus lose their identity in many cases. The technique of execution should be perfect.

The presentation of the wordsigns in the Ninth Lesson of the Manual is particularly useful for study both in reading and in writing. The "Review Exercise on Wordsigns" gives the forms for all the wordsigns up to this point, and the "key" furnishes the student the means of having someone dictate the wordsigns to him for practice and comparison. The student can make up a list of the additional wordsigns in the same way. The two lists should be written and rewritten, read and reread until complete mastery is secured. The skill in execution — the *habit* of writing quickly — acquired by the repetition practice on the simple wordsigns, will increase the speed in writing other words. Thus all the work done on a certain type of joining is cumulative in value.

Words of High Frequency. — Someone has wisely paraphrased and adapted the old saying "take care of the pennies and the dollars will take care of themselves" into "take care of the monosyllables and the polysyllables will take care of themselves." This is literally true, for the monosyllables make up a very large proportion of all written and spoken language. Mr. Leonard B. Ayres, in his book "A Measuring

Scale for Ability in Spelling," published by the Russell Sage Foundation, presents a list of the one thousand most frequently recurring words, from which the following are quoted:

Drill 1.—The fifty most common words

The, and, of, to, I, a, in, that, you, for, it, was, is, will, as, have, not, with, be, your, at, we, on, he, by, but, my, this, his, which, dear, from, are, all, me, so, one, if, they, had, has, very, were, been, would, she, or, there, her, an.

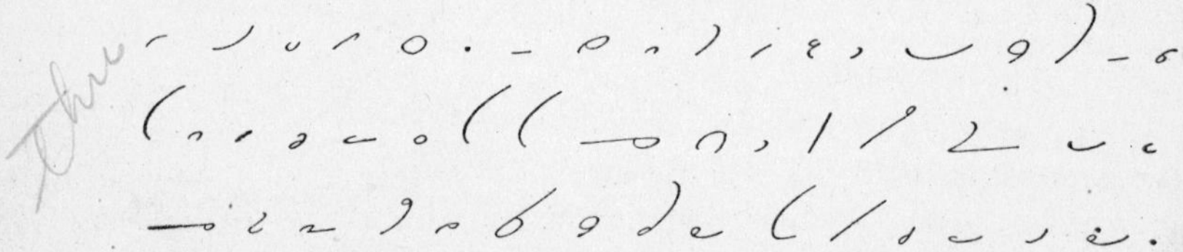

Drill 2.—The next fifty most common words

When, time, go, some, any, can, what, send, out, them, him, more, about, no, please, week, night, their, other, up, our, good, say, could, who, may, letter, make, write, thing, think, should, truly, now, its, two, take, thank, do, after, than, sir, last, house, just, over, then, work, day, here.

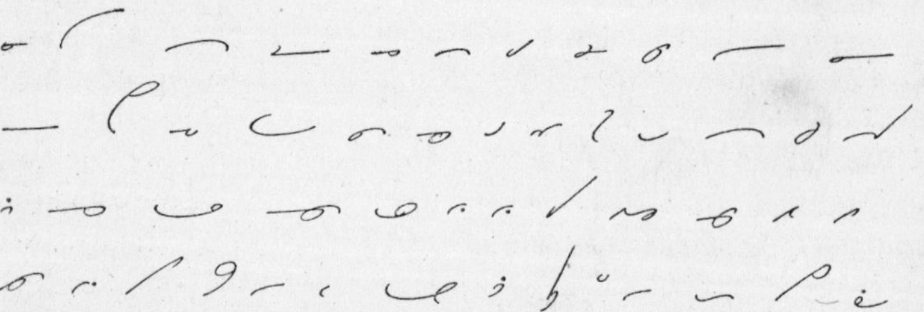

Note: The words "some," "night," "last," "just," and "over" are written according to advanced principles. "Truly" and "been" usually occur in phrases and are then abbreviated to "T" and "B".

BUSINESS LETTERS

13. (49)

14. (57)

15. (63)

16.

We-regret, owing, guides, files, delivery, on-the-date, in-your-letter, planning, to-send-the, of-next-month, I-regret, have-not-yet, kindly, cash, office, for-next-year, we-should-like, we-have-had, to-curtail, later, publication, combs, we-wish.

(61)

17.

25

(103)

18.

(101)

If-you-can, duplicate, thirty, dozen, mortgage, on-your, tenants, roof, leaks, every-time, do-so, if-you-will, leased, if-you-are-not, we-shall-have, to-ask, to-take-care, through, of-your-city, Lithia, water, we-trust-that, agents, blank, which-will, in-making, please-write-us.

SPEED STUDY X

TENTH LESSON

The Past Tense of Wordsigns. — The drill furnishes an opportunity to review the important regular verbs in the list.

Drill 1

Key: accepted, accorded, acknowledged, acquainted, advertised, allowed, arranged, assisted, avoided, believed, billed, called, cared, carried, caused, claimed, cleared, collected, considered, copied, corrected, covered, credited, dated, delivered, desired, determined, devoted, differed, drafted, educated, endured, existed, experienced, favored, followed, formed, governed, handed, improved, inclosed, influenced, insured, lighted, liked, looked, marketed, mortgaged, moved, named, objected, obliged, occasioned, occupied, ordered, organized, parted, pleased, pointed — appointed, published, purposed, questioned, received, recorded, referred, regarded, regretted, remarked, remitted, reported, represented, respected, returned, satisfied, sided, spirited, stated, stocked, suggested, thanked, timed, trusted, used, valued, wanted, wired, wondered, worded.

Joining the "t" for "ed." — After a few wordsigns, where the forms are distinctive, the joined stroke is used.

Drill 2

Key: asked, charged, effected, judged, wished, worked, checked, directed, booked.

An Exercise on "er" and "or." — The following drill gives the most common illustrations of this principle:

Drill 3

Key: acceptor, advertiser, believer, caller, carrier, changer, claimer, clearer, collector, corrector, creditor, customer, deliverer, director, educator, finder, follower, friendlier, fuller, giver, governor, instanter, insurer, keeper, kinder, letterer, lighter, looker, mover, namer, objector, obliger, organizer, outer, pointer, publisher, questioner, referrer, remarker, respecter, sender, shipper, sider, speaker, stater, suggester, surer, thinker, timer, user, valuer.

The Abbreviating Principle. — By studying and practicing the list of words written under the abbreviating principle given on pages 64, 65, and 66 of the Manual, the student will have at his command a good working vocabulary of most of the most common words that may be written by this principle. The mastery of this will also so firmly fix the principle in mind that the student will apply it to other words almost automatically. The best method of mastering these is to study each word carefully and practice the individual outline until it can be written rapidly. Practice reading the forms given on pages 65 and 66 until speed in reading is acquired. Then the entire list should be dictated and read back until it can be written rapidly.

"Dollar" Standing Alone. — When standing alone, "dollar" is expressed by "d-o." With "k" beneath, it expresses "dollar and a quarter"; with "f," "dollar and a half"; with the "cents" sign (above the line), "dollars and cents."

Drill 4

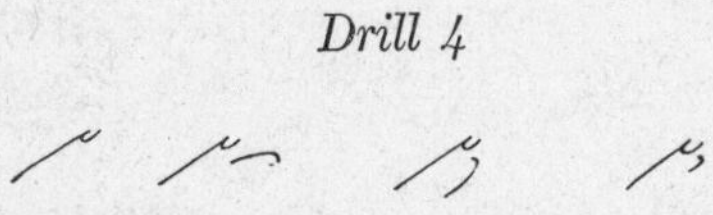

Key: dollar, dollar and a quarter, dollar and a half, dollars and cents.

BUSINESS LETTERS

19. 18 24.75 (48)

20. 7 20 (49)

21. 7 (47)

22. 7 1786 8.75 (73)

Many-thanks, this-will-be, officially, home-office, appreciate, courtesy, we-are-writing, we-received, wagon, therein, to-send-you, cheaper, to-get, and-make, from-them, books, balancing, on-which-date, for-which, charged, which-you-wish.

23. [shorthand] (71)

24. [shorthand] (76)

25. [shorthand] (86)

What-do-you, about-that, placed, with-us, impossible, you-mention, as-many, finance, season, of-any, canceled, of-next-year, possibly, through-the, and-note, you-make, in-these-matters, full, whenever, possible, you-can-find, for-us, therefore, assistance.

SPEED STUDY XI

ELEVENTH LESSON

Phrase-Writing — Elementary. — Phrase-writing has been well described as an "art within an art." There is no doubt that a great saving of time and effort is effected by judicious phrase-writing. The purpose of joining words is to eliminate the loss of time occasioned by lifting the pen and in passing from one shorthand form to another. The theory is that each pen-lift is equal to a stroke, and therefore that every word joined saves time equivalent to writing a stroke.

Limitations of Phrase-Writing. — This theory, however, is true only where there is no *hesitancy in joining the words.* Furthermore, it is not true of very long phrases, because such phrases destroy the rhythm of shorthand writing. There is no question about this: that a great saving of time is effected by joining the commonly occurring expressions.

The Kind of Phrases to Practice. — Phrases are of three kinds: (1) those which have been memorized and can be written fluently without conscious attention; (2) those which are devised from well-understood principles, such as "to-be," "as-well-as," "have-been," "you-do-not," etc.; (3) those which are improvised on the spur of the moment.

As phrase writing is an art, it is only by much experience that the student will gain a knowledge of just what words can be joined with safety and advantage, but this knowledge will be more quickly acquired through a close study of the examples given in the textbook than in any other way. At first it will be well to confine the phrasing to simple, common, everyday expressions consisting of not more than five strokes.

How to Practice Phrases. — Phrases, like wordsigns, are useful only if *thoroughly mastered*. The phrases illustrated in the Eleventh Lesson are among the most common phrases of the language, and the student should devote sufficient practice to them to be able to execute them with great rapidity and accuracy. A point to be remembered in executing phrases is that ultimately a phrase is *one compact thing*. Think of it as one word and it will be executed in that way. There should be no stop at the joinings. By thinking of *each word* separately there will be a tendency to stop at the end of each word, and facility in execution will thus be lost, but it is necessary while *learning* the long phrases to separate them into smaller units. If difficulty is experienced in executing some of the phrases consisting of several strokes, practice a part of the phrase at a time until the difficulties of that part have been removed. Then add a little more to it and so on until the whole phrase can be written without a perceptible stop. The following illustrations will make this clear:

you will be sorry to learn

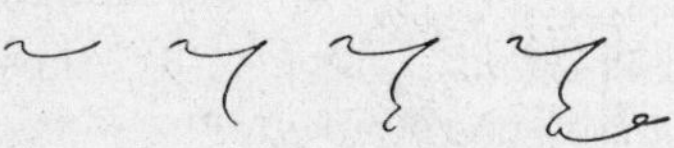

I would like to see

you will not be able

I have not been able

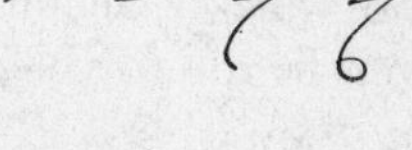

Drill 1

Practice each of the short phrases, such as "it-is," "of-the," "to-be," "with-this," given in the Eleventh Lesson of the Manual until it can be executed accurately at a very rapid speed. Read all the notes, repracticing any forms that are not well written. The elements of the short phrases need not be separated for practice as they present no very great executional difficulties.

Drill 2

The following additional phrases should be practiced in sections, and then in whole. The long phrases of the Manual should be included.

Practice in reading is just as important as writing.

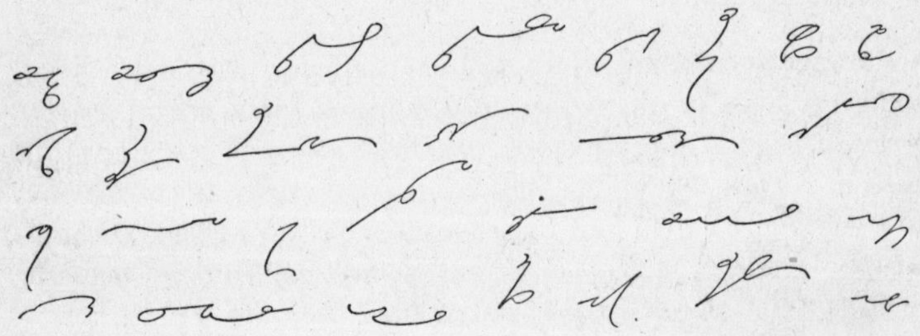

Key: we-are-sorry-to-say, we-regret-to-say, I-would-like-to-have, I-would-like-to-know, I-do-not-wish, we-have-not-been, I-hope-that, we-hope-to-hear, you-do-not-believe, for-the-first-time, several-months-ago, at-this-time, many-weeks-ago, you-don't-care, they-have-been, glad-to-know, to-become, to-day-or-to-morrow, we-told-him, we-are-in-receipt-of-your-letter, in-reference-to-this, the-goods, I-am-sorry-to-learn, recent-letter, suggest-that, in-order-to-be, several-days-ago, in-respect-to-the.

Colloquial Expressions. — It is often necessary to distinguish colloquial expressions, especially in writing testimony, poetry, or dialogue. Usually the contracted form of "not" can be represented by "nt," except, of course, in the case of "wasn't" where it is necessary to add the apostrophe. In other contractions, the apostrophe is used.

Drill 3

Key: couldn't, didn't, doesn't, haven't, hasn't, shouldn't, wouldn't, I'm, I'll, we'll, you'll, they're, it'll.

Phrase Vocabulary. — It will be well for the student to make up a list of all the common phrases to be found in the first ten lessons and add these to those given in the Eleventh Lesson. These should be used for practice in both reading and writing. By adding these phrases to the writing vocabulary a decided increase in speed will be noticed. Constant review of the phrases is necessary until they are written automatically. Dictation and reading of the notes are absolutely essential to a successful handling of the phrasing problem.

BUSINESS LETTERS

26. (46)

27. (52)

28. (53)

29. (54)

30.

For-which, we-are-sending-you, receipted, we-thank-you-for-the, courteous, to-our-letter, your-recent-letter, I-am-glad, that-the-order, designs, remainder, we-hope-that, entirely-satisfactory, absence, we-shall-draw, on-that-date, if-this-is-not, I-send-you, for-collection, against.

(58)

31.

(59)

32.

(72)

33.

(85)

Directory, from-him, with-reference-to-the-matter, few-days-ago, I-have-not-received, Dear-Mr., Phelps, we-are-in-receipt-of-your-letter, immediate-attention, we-are-sorry-to-say, pamphlets, you-may-have, to-wait, week-or-two, indeed, decree, Robert, Wallace, which-may-be, asked.

34.

(111)

35.

(105)

Looked, the-order, Albert, we-find, of-nails, hammers, called, should-have, reached, before-this, we-are-having, suggest, freight, original, promptly, Grant, quality, certainly, customers, we-sent, pairs, firm, Clinton, afternoon, wired.

SPEED STUDY XII

TWELFTH LESSON

Rounding Angles. — The numerous examples of angle joinings illustrated in the Twelfth Lesson of the Manual furnish an opportune time to introduce a principle in writing that has a vital influence on speed — the rounding of angles. The predominance of curves is fundamental in the system. It is this feature that gives to the writing its fluent and graceful appearance and adds tremendously to its speed possibilities. But angles do occur of necessity. In addition to furnishing a balancing point in the outline, they contribute greatly to the legibility of forms, if rightly handled. An angle, however, does not necessarily mean an abrupt stop, but, rather, a change in direction. Early in his practice the writer should form the habit of getting around the corners rapidly. A study of a page of notes of an expert writer will show that this idea has been developed to a remarkable degree. The GREGG WRITER in a recent number, when commenting on the notes of a stenographer who complained that he found it "impossible to get speed," said:

"The notes showed wonderful exactness of form, but the angles were so positive that it was evident that an absolute pause had taken place after each of them. Precision is a good thing, especially when learning the principles, but it can be carried too far in the case of rapid note-taking and thus prove a detriment to the acquirement of high speed. When the writer of shorthand has attained sufficient command over his hand to make the outlines rapidly and yet retain proportion of form, he should aim to acquire skill in turning the corners, so to speak — in other words, round off the angles. This is a point worthy of thought, experiment, and practice on the part of the writer who aims at becoming an expert."

Study the following examples illustrating the principle:

Drill 1

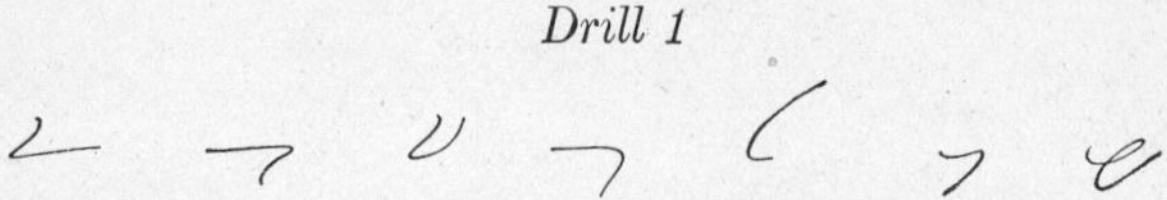

Key: from, important, found, much, been, refer, rapid.

It will be seen that the outlines preserve the distinctive forms and yet it is evident that no perceptible stop was made at the angle. To get around the angles in this rapid way requires a clear mental picture of the entire form, and a certain knack to execute the movement smoothly. It is easy to acquire this knack, and it is a very important factor in acquiring speed. The sharpness of the angle is simply avoided and the form executed without a stop, much as it is eliminated in such words as "friend" and "keep." The idea is not to make an effort to round the angle, but to eliminate the sharp point. The proportion and distinctive forms of the strokes must, however, be carefully preserved.

Drill 2

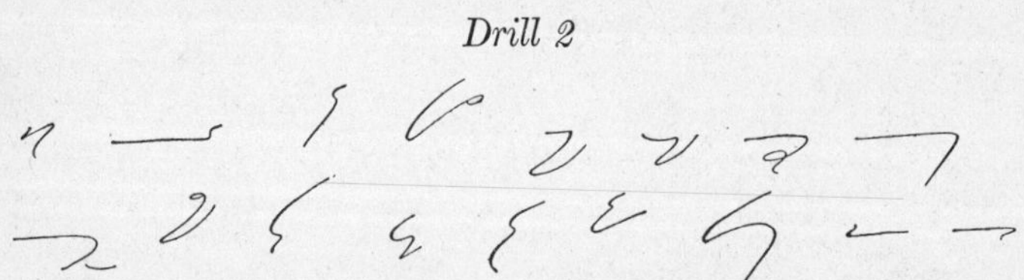

Key: stop, month, subject, badly, invent, refund, emphasis, manage, manufacturer, event, business, punched, public, speed, baggage, some, must.

The principle can be applied to phrasing also with advantage — and particularly to such blended phrases as the first five following:

Drill 3

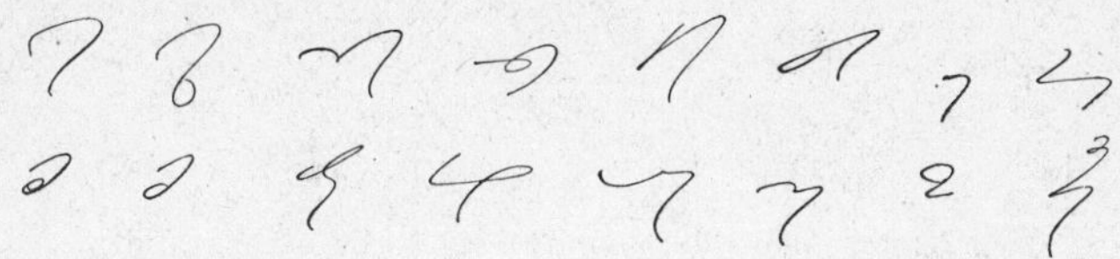

Key: would-have-been, would-have-been-able, could-have-been, might-have, which-would-have-been, I-would-be, in-which, from-which, to-find, to-favor, what-has-been, which-may-be, will-not-be, cannot-be, I-shall-not, we-have-not-been.

Drill 4

The Reading and Writing Exercises on page 87 of the Manual will afford an excellent drill in applying the principle of rounding angles. Copy each exercise several times until the forms are well memorized. Then have the whole dictated until it can be written swiftly without stops.

BUSINESS LETTERS

36.

(37)

37.

(48)

38.

(54)

39.

(55)

40.

If-you-will-send-us, blank, school, topics, teaches, texts, great-favor, product, Green, appropriation, permit, advantage, offer, to-offer, basis, quotations, please-note, f.o.b., previously, quoted, manager, foundry, tells, merchandise, factory, upon-receipt, distance, reverse, charges, plot.

(65)

41.

(66)

42.

(70)

43.

(72)

Obtain, shares, Carpenter, several-days-ago, promised, very-soon, slides, if-possible, in-spite, it-is-not, of-next-week, large-number, standard, sufficient, quantities, we-hope-that-this, inconvenience, in-order-that, to-check, records, indicate, if-there-is, correction.

PASS IT ON

—*Waldo Pondray Warren* (184)

You-think, might-be, to-some, otherwise, clip, it-would-be, to-encourage, employees, especially, among-those, hundreds, suggestions, magazines, snowflakes, any-one, persons, observations, virtually, benefit, discovered, points, adapt, to-my, I-found, I-wanted, clipping.

SPEED STUDY XIII

THIRTEENTH LESSON

Building Up a Working Vocabulary. — It will be well for the student to take four or five words illustrating each principle — selecting the most frequently recurring words — and practice these until skill in using the suffixes has been acquired. Each group of words thus mastered will form a nucleus for all words of the same class. This practice should be followed through the remaining lessons of the Manual.

Size of Shorthand Characters. — Nothing perhaps adds so much to speed and ease of execution as a size of notes that is adapted to the individual. In shorthand as much depends upon manual skill as upon mental activity, and the highest achievement depends upon a harmonious, rhythmical co-operation of the two.

It is obvious that all persons cannot write notes of uniform size. It would be as reasonable to set a measure for a stride in walking or running. The characteristics of the individual must therefore be taken into account. But while the size may vary with the individual, the proportion of one character to another should always be maintained. In no other way can *accuracy* be acquired.

In determining the size of notes there is one bit of advice that cannot lead you astray — don't write large, sprawling notes. Other things being equal, a small note is better than a large one, for the reason that the greater the distance the hand travels, the more rapid must be its speed. If the hand is moving rapidly, control of it is not so easily maintained as when writing at a slower speed, and in consequence the notes will lose in symmetry. At the beginning of the study, make the characters small and accurate; they will very likely increase somewhat in size when you begin to take dictation. If you have had considerable training in penmanship, the notes should be in keeping with the size of your longhand letters. Avoid a cramped style as much as you would a large one. Make a close study of your notes and adopt a size that is adapted to your hand, but if there is any doubt in your mind select the smallest possible size *you can execute with freedom of movement*.

The Studies in the earlier lessons provide much valuable material for practice, and the student should aim to incorporate the characteristics of the examples in his writing. He will soon find that he is acquiring a grace of motion in writing and a comfortable feeling of being unhampered by mechanical difficulties that is as gratifying to the mind as it is conducive to speed in writing.

Value of Compactness. — Writing on this subject, the accomplished shorthand reporter, H. W. Thorne, said:

> "Acquire the habit of writing neatly and compactly. This conduces to speed. Large, sprawling outlines have the opposite tendency.
>
> The argument that small characters produce a cramped action of the hand, and, hence result in loss of speed, while a large, free, swinging style carries the writer forward with "leaps and bounds," thereby enhancing speed, was effectually controverted a quarter of a century ago."

The illustration following is intended to show the difference between small, compact notes and large, widely spaced writing:

Small, Compact Notes.—Correct Style

The dotted lines show the direct line of travel from one outline to another.

Large, Sprawling Notes.—Incorrect Style

The dotted lines, indicating the trail of the pen, show how little attention was paid to economy in movement by spacing the outlines far apart, by waste motion between outlines, and by not considering the point at which the next outline begins.

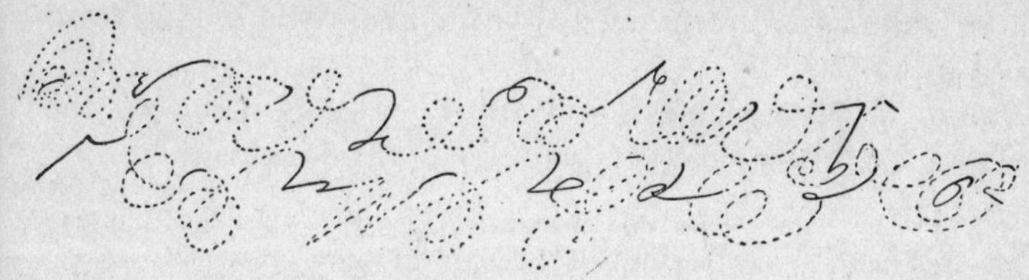

The elimination of unrecorded movements—as indicated by dotted lines in the foregoing—should receive the very earnest attention of students.

BUSINESS LETTERS

44. (40)

45. (50)

46. (58)

47. (60)

48.

To-inform-you, I-have-taken, within-a-few-days, Independent, Soda, Fountain-Company, urging, at-our-office, and-make-the, arrangements, confirmation, 1800 bushels, White, bought, premium, sold, we-thank-you-for, we-have-not-heard, in-response, to-our-letters, anyone-else, can-make.

(59)

49. (65)

50. (71)

51.

Will-you-please, inform-us, within, mentioned, first-of-the-month, we-are-unable, that-it-was, addressed, duplicating, Graham, will-you-please-see, as-soon-as-you-can, Raymond, has-not-been, for-the-past, to-discontinue, he-should-be, ten-days-ago, you-asked, to-assist, charter, I-sent-you.

(83)

52.

(90)

53.

(135)

Since-then, what-is-the, in-fact, you-have-done, excellent, engravers, we-will-mail, if-you-have-not, some-day, in-a-day-or-two, at-any-rate, I-should-like-to-have, final, decision, to-match, if-you-decide, we-will-make, liberal, allowance, guarantee.

THE SECRET BLOTTING PAD

Harper's Weekly (186)

Foreign, acts, that, alert, infinite, precautions, baffle, blotting, quite, jealously, holding, in-front, mirror, commercial, forgotten, existence, British, sand, shaker, specially, expedient, absorbent, roller, this-was, tried, up-and-down, once-or-twice, cleverest, attempt, to-decipher.

SPEED STUDY XIV

FOURTEENTH LESSON

The Technique of Writing. — A point to be observed in writing such words as "contribute," "intervene," "intelligence," etc., is to start far enough above the line of writing to give the full-length stroke its proper length. For example, the base of *b*, *v*, and *j* in the foregoing words should rest on the line of writing. Observe the following examples (the dotted line represents the line of writing):

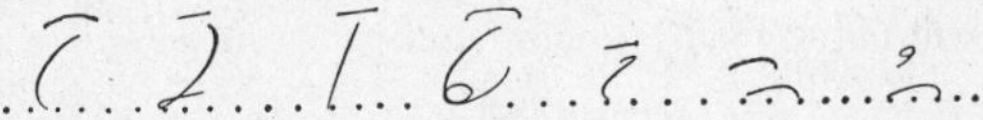

Key: contribute, intervene, intelligence, contraband, interrupt, contract, extract.

Learn to pass directly from the prefix to the rest of the word without any "pen motions in the air" or stops. Place the prefix so you will have the shortest possible distance to travel in starting the remaining part of the outline.

A little special attention should be given to the formation of the prefixes "agri," "anti," and "incli." The loop should be made perfectly distinct and the sizes of circles made positive. Study the following:

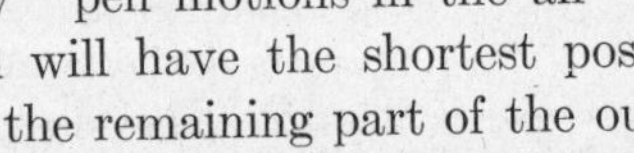

Key: aggravation, antipathy, include.

Do not neglect the practice on the compound prefixes.

The Value of Reading Ability. — The ability to read one's notes is of even greater importance than the ability to write. That this is a well-recognized fact is attested by the number of articles that have been written on the subject. One of the best teachers of shorthand has this to say:

"A great amount of writing from dictation every day and continuously with no further thought but to write, and write rapidly, is often mistaken for general improvement. I believe students in general would rather perform this one small task than any other, and the task which seems the most difficult to perform, in the proper manner, is for the student to sit down quietly, and alone, and read over a long article which has just been written. Few students there are who have the grit to do it. The common way is for half a dozen or more to join forces and together hash over the pages, first one suggesting a word, and then another. This is a great mistake, and the more the student indulges in it the more certain he may be that he will fail to read his notes alone when he accepts a position."

Another teacher and writer says:

"If teachers would compel learners to read clear, accurately written or printed shorthand as they progress with the study of the textbook, and continue the practice during the entire shorthand course, there would be a marked increase in speed and a wonderful facility in the transcription of notes. It is important that students should be able to read their writing fluently, but if they are confined to the practice exclusively they will develop personal peculiarities that will lead them away from the clear, facile standard outlines of printed shorthand that will eventually render their writing difficult to be read by others, if not whclly illegible. . . . When this plan is more generally adopted we will hear less of 'sticking places' and more of those who are making steady progress from the day of enrollment to the day of graduation."

Fred H. Gurtler, the well-known shorthand reporter of Chicago, says: "Nothing contributes more readily to a good shorthand vocabulary than the reading of well-written shorthand."

The practice should be of two kinds: First, the reading of well-written shorthand that approaches as closely as possible to absolute accuracy. This is for the purpose of creating correct ideals. Such writing may be found in the outlines, phrases, and continuous passages of the textbook, and the exercises in this book — as well as the plates in the GREGG WRITER. All of these are *actually written notes* — models which the student should aim to imitate.

Second, your own notes taken from dictation. The latter is by far the most important for the reason that no matter how expert you become in writing, your notes will vary to some extent from the ideal forms. These differences can be learned only by analyzing and reading your own notes. Reading carefully written shorthand will not aid you in this. This work should be supplemented by reading the notes of your teacher and fellow students.

Correcting While Reading. — The time to correct your shorthand, and to add to your shorthand vocabulary the forms that have given you trouble in writing, is *when you read.* In reading, encircle every outline that has caused you the slightest hesitation and devote some special practice to executing it until the movement has been mastered. Rupert P. SoRelle, in his book "Expert Shorthand Speed Course," emphasizes this point. He says:

"Every outline that varies from the correct form or causes hesitation in reading should be the subject of special practice. In this way troublesome outlines will gradually disappear, and all the frequently recurring words will soon become so familiar that they can be written rapidly and with precision."

BUSINESS LETTERS

54. (58)

55. (69)

56. (67)

57.

I-have-sent-you, Metropolitan, by-express, as-soon-as-these, lowest, patterns, some-time-ago, any-of-these, are-now, out-of-stock, if-you-have, on-the-subject, would-like-to-know, furnish-us, George, in-this-case, notified, Thomas, Hughes, hospital, district, provisions.

5375 ... 05 ... 358 ... 07 ... (85)

58. ... (82)

59. ...

Revised, chapter, restored, proceedings, to-conduct, defense, Richard, Brown, Public, Electric-Company, we-send, protection, restrictive, construction, located, electric-power, you-will-be-glad, this-information, Dayton, material, booklet, about-them, we-hope-to-be-able.

(106)

60.

(112)

61.

(126)

Members, advanced, kindly-inform-us, in-connection-with-the, kindly-give-me, if-you-will-write, about-its, we-shall-not-be-able, for-the-reason, from-us, excessive, you-are-now, undoubtedly, to-purchase, additional, within-the, two-or-three-months, which-you-have, in-our-files.

THE OBJECT OF LITERARY CULTURE

John Morley (185)

Literary, culture, at-the-present-time, counteract, dominant, tendencies, pursuits, evil, habits, ardent, preserve, devote, as-much-time, performance, investigation, gifts, wealth, can-never, opulence, human-being, confined, promoted, adherence, generous, purest, rectitude.

SPEED STUDY XV

FIFTEENTH LESSON

The Law of Rhythm in Shorthand Writing

By John Robert Gregg in the Gregg Writer

In the course of an informal talk to a "speed class" some time ago, we were asked by the teacher to express our views about the value of phrase-writing. The teacher seemed to be surprised, and perhaps disappointed, at the tenor of our remarks. We afterwards learned that he had devoted a great deal of time to the study of phrasing and had constantly impressed upon his students that a mastery of phrase-writing was the open sesame to verbatim reporting speed. There was a time when we held that view — before we had an understanding of what we might term the law of rhythm in shorthand writing. Before discussing that law, we wish to repeat the substance of what we said to the class:

1. That simple, natural phrasing is of immense value in the attainment of a high degree of stenographic skill.
2. That involved phrases, that is, phrases requiring much mental effort to recall, or much continuous manual effort to execute, are a hindrance instead of a help.
3. That under stress of rapid writing the reporter generally reverts to simple, natural forms, even if they are somewhat lengthy.

In support of our theories, we stated that an examination of the actual notes of skilled reporters of all systems — and this includes those who have distinguished themselves in the various speed contests — will show that when writing under pressure, or where the work is long sustained, they seldom use any but the simple and natural phrases. There are several reasons for this:

Long phrases impose on the reporter such a degree of concentration of mind and of precision in writing that they become irksome in a long siege of note-taking. It is true that there are exceptions to this in the case of some young reporters who take a peculiar delight in phrase-writing, and who have made that phase of shorthand writing a special hobby.

Another reason is that there is a law of rhythm in shorthand writing. Every writer of shorthand, for instance, spaces between forms with almost mechanical uniformity. The spacing may be close or wide according to the habit of the writer, but it will be *uniform* in width, and retain that uniformity even under extreme pressure.

In a similar way, the hand and mind become accustomed to making just about so many motions or efforts at a time, and when the writing goes much beyond the *average,* as in the case of a very long phrase, the rhythm is destroyed. When this happens a certain amount of time is lost before the momentum or fluency of motion is recovered. It is well to have this point fully understood, as it will explain why diligent practice on some fascinating phrase-forms does not seem to produce the expected result in the way of increased skill in writing.

Here is a shorthand illustration that may help to make this clear:

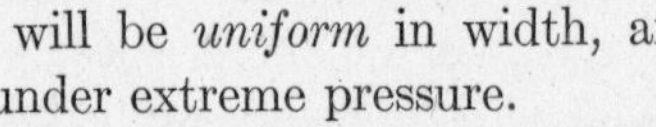

Key: Thanking you for your kind attention to this matter, and hoping to hear from you at an early date, I remain Yours very truly.

This phrase-form contains twenty-four words, and it is a common enough expression. Even with the ordinary variations of it — such as the omission of "kind," or the substitution of "again" for "at an early date" — the words can all be joined without any trouble. It is, too, a fluent, easy-running combination, as it is all along the line.

And yet it is *not* a good, practical phrase-form. Why? Simply because there are so many continuous movements in executing it that the hand is liable to get "blind staggers" while writing it, especially under the pressure of actual work. This will be readily understood, but it is not so generally understood that the introduction of a phrase-form *requiring sustained effort* is *followed* by hesitancy or loss of momentum. The natural rhythm is broken, and the hand has to adjust itself to the usual average of effort. Let us split the foregoing phrase-form into what may be considered its natural divisions, and see the result:

Key: Thanking you for — kind attention — this matter — and hoping — hear from you — at an early date — I remain Yours very truly.

Here you find that the balance or rhythm is preserved. There are a few easy movements (none of them over four pen motions), then a lift of the pen, and a fresh start. That is what we mean by rhythm in writing.

This illustration may possibly aid in conveying the idea we have in mind. We confess that we find it difficult to express it so that it will not be regarded as a condemnation of phrasing. We most emphatically believe in the value of phrase-writing of the *right* kind; but many writers waste a great deal of time and effort in the concoction of long phrase-forms that are an actual hindrance to the attainment of speed. If the time and effort so spent had been devoted to *more intense practice on the simple, natural phrase-forms*, their progress would have been much greater.

Nothing is gained, then, by striving after long and involved phrases, but a great deal is gained by persistent drill on the common, everyday phrases that occur in all kinds of matter. The trouble is that students, and even advanced writers, do not realize the necessity for practice on phrase-forms with which they are thoroughly familiar. "Familiarity breeds contempt," as it were. It is only when they see the wonderful celerity with which these phrases are written by the highly skilled writer that they are induced to give them the attention they deserve. The greatest reporters and the most expert writers, as a rule, have acquired an admirable command over all common phrases and wordforms, but they have not used the ingeniously brief contractions which have such a fascination for the amateur writer. Under pressure, the mind and hand revert to those forms which require very little effort to recall and which can be written with little regard to exactitude.

There are three definite steps to be taken in the acquirement of speed in shorthand: First, mastery of the alphabetic combinations; second, mastery of the simple words that constitute more than fifty per cent of all ordinary matter; third, mastery of the common phrases.

And by *mastery* we mean the ability to write combinations, common words, and common phrases with great rapidity while preserving proportion or accuracy of form. This ability can be attained only by much systematic, concentrated practice.

BUSINESS LETTERS

62. 129 ... 15 ... (56)

63. 24 ... 18 24 ... 29 ... (81)

64. 10 ... (80)

65.

Overlooked, to-meet, welcome, item, drawn, First-National-Bank, of-this-city, transit, we-wrote-you, to-furnish-us, issuance, this-delay, annoying, with-thanks, comply, we-take, similar, continually, to-confine, newspapers, of-large, circulation, include, Postal, Motor, Service, operating, trucks.

(83)

66.

(96)

67.

(99)

Day-and-night, transportation, of-mail, anticipates, that-there-may-be, occasional, breakdown, mechanics, appliances, misunderstandings, which-could-have-been, bank, hear-from-you, I-thank-you-for, I-understand, Camden, I-shall-be-able, I-shall-send.

68.

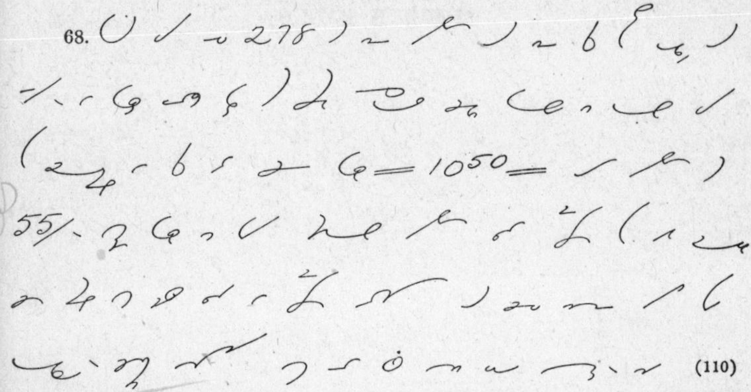

(110)

69.

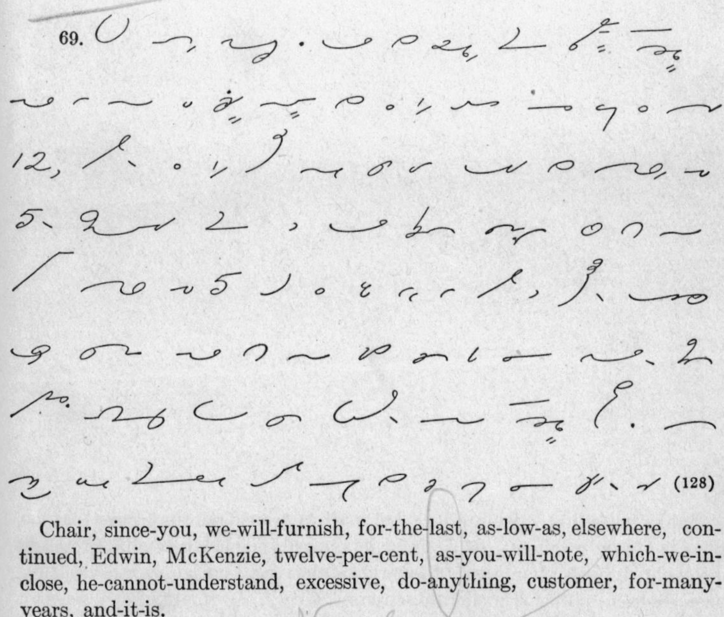

(128)

Chair, since-you, we-will-furnish, for-the-last, as-low-as, elsewhere, continued, Edwin, McKenzie, twelve-per-cent, as-you-will-note, which-we-inclose, he-cannot-understand, excessive, do-anything, customer, for-many-years, and-it-is.

MODERN BANKS

Selected (180)

Banks, absolute, transaction, borrowing, transferring, from-place-to-place, provide, accuracy, dispatch, benches, market-place, prevails, oriental, insolvent, broken, bankrupt, formerly, exclusively, corporations, wealthy, business-men, patrons, moderate, circumstances, convenient, courtesies.

SPEED STUDY XVI

SIXTEENTH LESSON

"Less" and "Ness." — These suffixes are written in full after a vowel, or where the use of the suffix-form would suggest a different word:

Drill 1

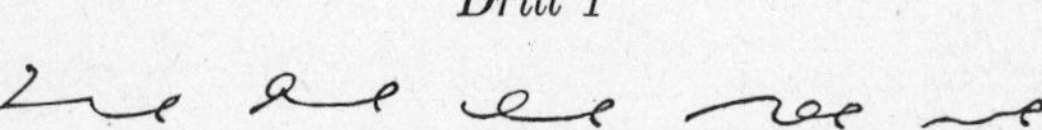

Key: formless, tireless, rayless, grayness, correctness.

If written with the suffix, the forms for these words might suggest *formal, tile, rail, grain, crown.*

It is sometimes necessary to disjoin the suffix after word-signs in order to secure distinctive outlines:

Drill 2

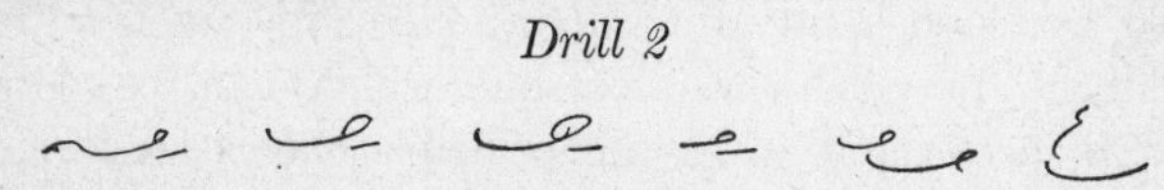

Key: clearness, likeness, lightness, nearness, regardless, speechless.

Review Practice. — Speed in shorthand is simply familiarity with the shorthand characters, and fast writing is not remarkable if shorthand is learned as well as longhand. The student of shorthand should be careful to learn the shorthand principles thoroughly. He can observe the thoroughness of his knowledge of the principles when he writes from dictation. He should not allow any error to go uncorrected when reading his notes.

In reviewing his notes he should see that the characters are well formed, and that they are of proper relative length. A short exercise should be written from dictation at a rate which will not crowd or hurry the writer, and which will allow him to make good notes. The student should then read the notes, correcting the mistakes in execution or application of the principle. He should write the exercise over and over again, until he can write it at a high rate of speed.

If the student cannot think of the outline given by the author of his system, or the one that is in his textbook, let him understand the principles so well that he can immediately construct the outline according to principle.

The student, in reading his notes, should seldom ask for assistance when puzzled, and the reader should not help him out too soon. — *Thomas P. Wilson.*

Off-Hand Word-Writing. — As a means of averting sluggish habits of mind and hand, and a most important discipline in other respects, nothing can be more beneficial to the student than to write off-hand, from dictation, words upon which he has had no previous practice but which can be correctly written in accordance with the principles he is learning or is supposed to have mastered. These exercises cannot be too copious, if the words be properly chosen. — *David Wolfe Brown.*

Drill and Review on Off-Hand Word-Writing

The following words are intended as a review of principles and to afford practice in off-hand word-writing. They should first be dictated, then compared with the shorthand outlines, corrections made and re-dictated:

1

2

3

4

5

6

7

8

9

10

Key: (1) electric, fashioned, coal, perquisite, art, uneasy, magnificent, intellect, retributive, slowness, (2) curtain, leisure, abstract, self-interest, restraint, commonly, detract, simple, divide, (3) expire, ounce, altogether, alternate, deflection, oppose, supreme, Farnsworth, thyself, exult, patron, (4) lawful, adjure, McLean, bequest, acute, material, central, friendliness, incline, (5) instruction, contract, basis, themselves, share, exclamation, esquire, announce, fuse, further, susceptible, (6) literary, inflection, overdone, circular, imposition, agriculture, heated, ascribe, treasure, (7) silk, cheers, subway, foreman, depend, improvise, surprise, inner, almost, (8) concern, finally, decision, assert, quick, crush, near, passage, agitation, instances, tendency, (9) useless, manners, someone, signed, etiquette, ulterior, genuine, defense, (10) funny, intention, adventure, yon, easily, swear, ground, earth, perhaps, rank.

BUSINESS LETTERS

70. (49)

71. (50)

72. (58)

73. (61)

Estimates, at-any-time, woodwork, require, established, Wentworth, has-taken, territory, if-you-want, flour, treatment, replying-to-your-inquiry, we-have-not-yet, Hubert, Osborne, we-have-not-been-able, railroad-company, on-account-of-the, embargo, safeguard, thoughtfully.

74. (62)

75. (66)

76. (66)

77.

To-your-inquiry, Hamilton, Kingston, one-hundred-dollars, entire-satisfaction, deposited, three-thousand-dollars, Alfred, Ward, cashier-of-the-bank, assigned, this-note, for-that-reason, Farnsworth, supply, we-expect, Decatur, under-contract, rosin, requirements, shortly.

(96)

78.

(92)

79. 1055 128 320 4,

(94)

Next-year's, consumption, we-are-in-a-position, to-quote, concentrating, yards, to-make, prompt, Simpson, I-wish, delightful, Current, Club, who-asked, orchestra, indication, in-the-near-future, we-have-your, indorsement, in-which-you-state, for-one-year, as-the-rate, reduction,

THE YOUNG MAN IN BUSINESS

George B. Cortelyou (200)

It-seems-to-me, young-man, emphasized, honesty, broadest, fullest, significance, possesses, achieved, men, scrupulous, standards, conduct, unfortunately, methods, primary, virtues, little-or-no, hardened, shriveled, struggle, no-one, fearful, cost, human, social, betterment.

SPEED STUDY XVII

SEVENTEENTH LESSON

It will be seen from the illustrations in the Manual that the disjoined suffixes are placed close to the ending of the preceding part of the word. The suffix should be so placed that the pen will have to travel the least possible distance. Another point to be observed is that the disjoined suffixes are single-effort characters and should be written with great accuracy until the movement used in executing them in this way has become a habit.

Analogical Abbreviation. — In the Twelfth Lesson of the Manual there are presented some fine examples of analogy in the treatment of frequently recurring syllables. The principle is so simple in theory that no explanation of it is needed, but since "drill," after all, is the next important thing to a thorough understanding of the principles, an additional exercise on words employing these and other frequently recurring sounds will be helpful.

Drills

"Age." —

Key: adage, bandage, bondage, lineage, luggage, foliage, marriage, courage, vantage, wreckage, package, baggage, cottage, leakage, village, homage.

"Ort," "Ord." —

Key: retort, contort, distort, extort, escort, cohort, discord, concord, lord, cord, exhort, ordinary, ordinance, ordain, ordnance, ordeal.

"Tal," "Tual," "Ture." —

Key: fatal, metal, recital, mental, rental, refutal, mortal, immortal, perpetual, habitual, effectual, actual, mutual, ritual, mature, armature, stature, furniture, capture.

"Uation," "Uition." —

Key: graduation, attenuation, extenuation, insinuation, continuation, fruition, tuition, intuition.

Quick Transitions. — Time may be lost during the pen-lifts, not only by unnecessary motions, but by performing necessary motions in a sluggish way. The movements of the hand in passing from word to word, from line to line, from page to page, may be performed in the right way, but not with sufficient alertness. "Quick transitions" should be the watchword of every writer who aims at speed. — *David Wolfe Brown.*

BUSINESS LETTERS

80. [shorthand] (53)

81. [shorthand] (61)

82. [shorthand] (69)

83. [shorthand]

Telegram, we-hope-that-these, the-delay, in-our-order, fumed, chiffonier, has-lost, to-order, recall, about-this-matter, insuring, Smelting, has-had, so-much, intention, inspection, representative, tour, we-shall-give, promise, evidently, never, notification, which-was, sent-you.

(71)

84.

(72)

85.

(74)

86.

Bottom, another-day, just, we-are-prepared, in-accordance-with-your, request, I-am-sending-you, I-have-seen, articles, justified, to-prepare, salable, we-have-been, compelled, to-pass, prominent, for-the-order, regulations, on-account-of-its.

(80)

87.

(90)

88.

(107)

Prohibitive, King, Snyder, exceedingly, in-full, purchases, some-weeks-ago, detailed, so-long-past-due, best-attention, damage, delivered, clearly, left, in-good-condition, and-was, clerk, responsibility, you-will-be-able, and-that-the, adjusted, help-you, notify, forwarded.

89.

(224)

I-wish-that, I-could-become, I-am-confident, mutual, result, casual, visits, contact, in-my, territory, we-meet, ideas, problems, smaller, towns, enter-credits, they-do-not, each-man, specialize, more-or-less, he-should-have, he-can-get, register, you-ask-me, some-of-these-days, margin.

BUSINESS HABITS

Rupert P. SoRelle (191)

Businesslike, demands, promptness, faithfulness, tidiness, determination, ability, on-time, efficiently, clock, in-your-work, absolutely, with-yourself, someone, estimated, girl, spends, school, actually, better-than, efficiency, for-the-day, multitude, of-little, affects, taking-up, renders.

SPEED STUDY XVIII

EIGHTEENTH LESSON

"Act," "Ect," "Ict," "Uct," "Sist," "Ist," etc. —

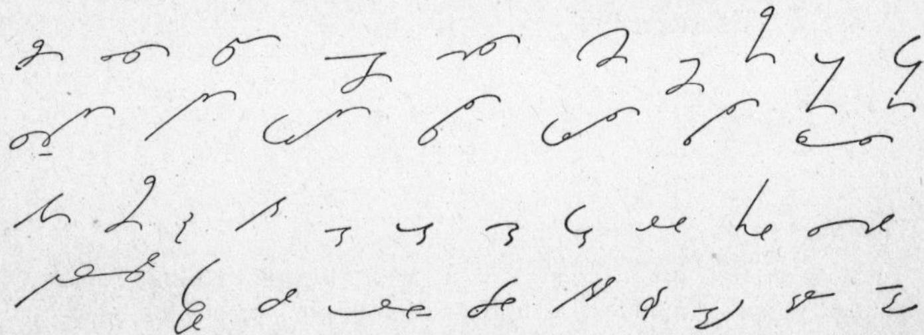

Key: exact, enact, attract, impact, contact, defect, infect, eject, reject, project, aqueduct, deduct, product, addict, predict, edict, select, depict, evict, subsist, desist, insist, resist, consist, persist, theorist, jurist, egotist, dramatist, Baptist, artist, linguist, pianist, disaster, cessation, incessant, cistern, intercessor.

"Mal," "Nal," "Ral." —

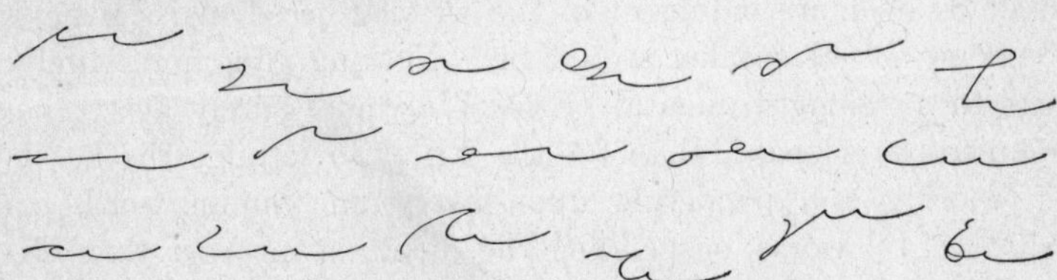

Key: dismal, informal, canal, arsenal, cardinal, marginal, nominal, ordinal, criminal, admiral, plural, coral, floral, temporal, corporal, federal, spiral.

"Ld." —

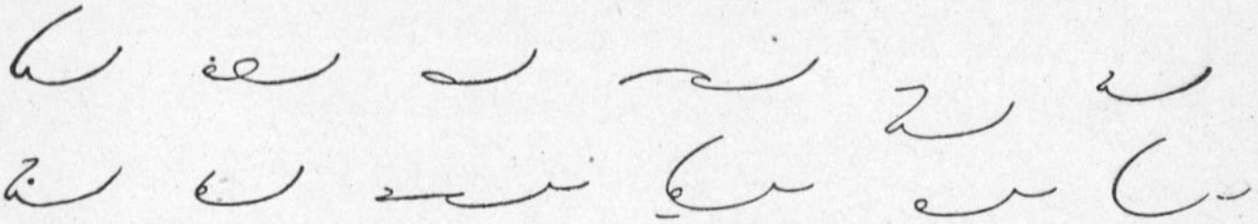

Key: bold, herald, yield, gold, unfold, sold, uphold, shield, smolder, bewi'der, elder, builder.

"Est," "Estation." —

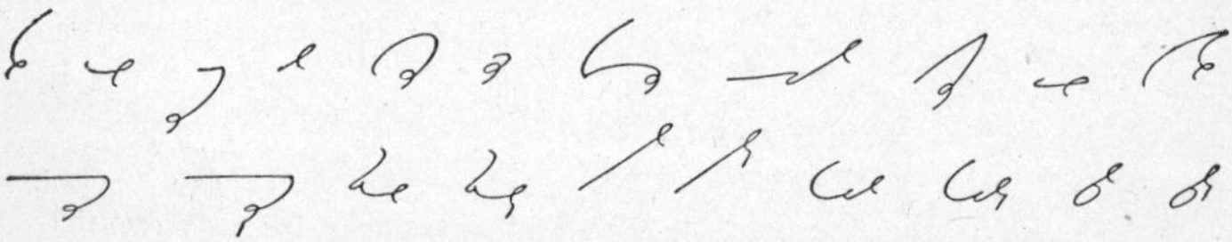

Key: best, rest, invest, test, divcst, west, biggest, modest, digest, honest, tempest, manifest, manifestation, forest, forestation, detest, detestation, protest, protestation, attest, attestation.

"Keep On." — In writing from dictation, it should be an invariable rule never to allow one's self to pause when a difficult or doubtful word or phrase is encountered. It should be understood that whenever the rate of dictation has been settled, the reader shall mercilessly proceed at that rate, and shall be no more indulgent of the writer's occasional slowness than an actual speaker would be. Nothing can more surely lead to a "sluggish mental process" or more surely delay the acquisition of speed, than for the writer to indulge the habit of pausing and pondering upon every uncommon word, or what is still worse, suspending the dictation in order that his doubts as to an outline may be settled by reference to a dictionary or a textbook. "Keep on" should be the inflexible rule for writer and reader. — *David Wolfe Brown.*

BUSINESS LETTERS

90. 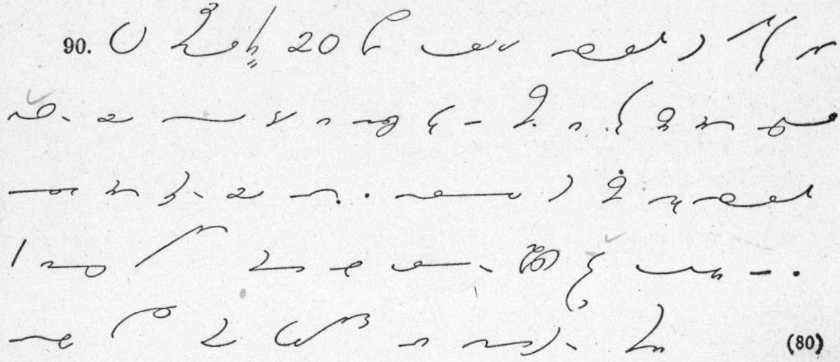 (80)

91. 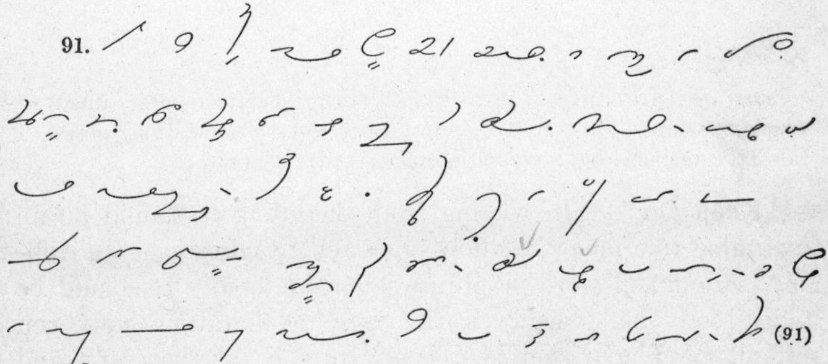 (91)

92. 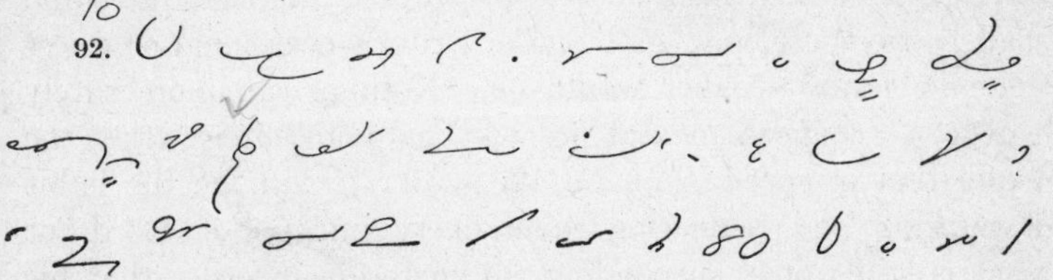

We-have-your-letter, lithographed, calendars, distribution, in-any-way, credit-memorandum, half-the, deduct, products, community, very-cordially-yours, Automatic, Furniture-Company, voucher, Atlantic, Coffee-Company, Raisin, Valley, Irrigation-Company, holdings, assessment.

(108)

93.

(113)

94.

Hold, medium, we-feel, statistics, enable, unrented, conference, we-had, I-have-decided, drayman, drayage, charged, exceptions, in-the, acknowledge-receipt-of-your-letter, Lockworth, selling, second, I-had, anticipated, averse, obligating.

(123)

95.

(148)

Indebtedness, pursued, we-did, I-think-that, bonds, in-need, drainage, owners, to-provide, Walter, McAdoo, Saxon, from-any, obligations, commissions, under-his, of-rebate, agreement, is-received, refunding, they-have-been, reserve, you-should, subagent, critical.

96.

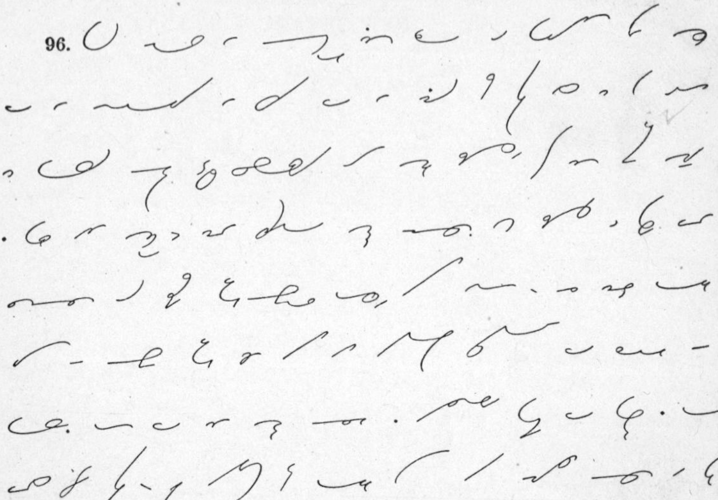

(222)

Carload, yard, plant, systematically, analyzed, quote, vital, considerations, based, economic, efficient, operation, machinery, deliberate, idleness, means, decreased, discover, to-avoid, repetition, proved, installations, under-separate-cover, catalog, entitled, executive, photographs, to-give-you.

NEW IDEAS

Madison C. Peters **(179)**

Idea, startling, danger, overmastering, minority, Fulton, launched, Hudson, asylum, enemy, Morse, telegraph, girdle, omnipresent, Charles, Goodyear, struggled, India, pawned, wife's, jewelry, starving, criticized, behold, vulcanized, over-five-hundred, Franklin, clouds, sneeringly.

SPEED STUDY XIX

NINETEENTH LESSON

Special Phrases — "Morning," "Night," "Sunday." — The word "morning" is represented by "mn-ing," and "night" by "ni." These forms lend themselves to very easy and useful phrases, as will be seen in the following:

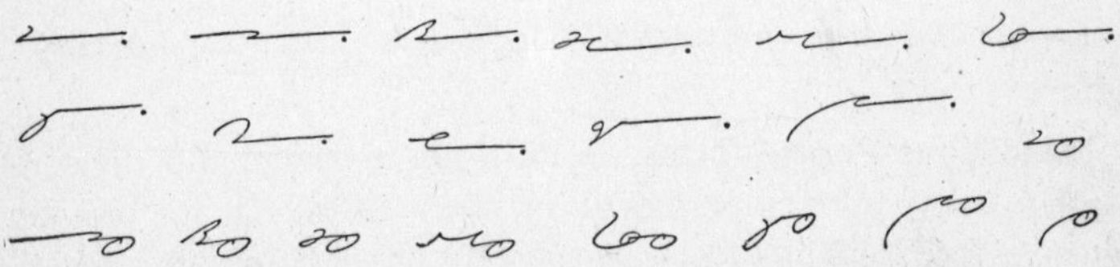

Key: Sunday-morning, Monday-morning, Tuesday-morning, Wednesday-morning, Thursday-morning, Friday-morning, Saturday-morning, this-morning, next-morning, yesterday-morning, to-morrow-morning, Sunday-night, Monday-night, Tuesday-night, Wednesday-night, Thursday-night, Friday-night, Saturday-night, to-morrow-night, to-night.

Railroad Phrases. — Among the railroad phrases in which the principle of intersection is used there are:

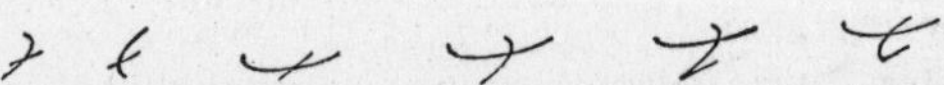

Key: freight-train, passenger-train, local-train, local-freight, local-freight-train, local-passenger-train.

Blended Phrases. — See also page 73, Drill 3.

Key: to-do, to-me, ought-to-know, ought-to-make, it-is-said, it-is-certain, it-was-said, it-was-certain, you-can-judge.

Modification of Wordforms. — Among the special modifications which are of frequent occurrence, the following may be added to those given in the Manual:

Key: rather-than, greater-than, longer-than, larger-than, sooner-than.

Injudicious Phrase-forms. — Phrasing in shorthand depends largely upon the temperament of the writer. In its broader sense, much of it has to be learned by observation and experience. There are general principles underlying the whole fabric, but the application of these must be left to a great extent to the writer. Phrasing can easily be carried to the extreme and it can also be injudicious in other ways. The study of the writing of young writers, particularly, discloses phrases which to the experienced eye are either unsafe or are not advisable from the practical standpoint. The Manual lays down the general rules in paragraph 72. In one paragraph it says: "The prepositions *to*, *of*, *in*, and *with*, and the conjunction *and* are generally joined to the words they precede, as *to-have*, *of-which*, *in-case*, *with-this*, *and-there*."

But in students' notes we have studied we find these: "expected me-to spend," "if you care-to look."

The phrases "me-to" and "care-to" violate the foregoing rule, and they are not *natural* phrases either in speaking or in writing. The phrases "to-spend" and "to-look" are natural and easy.

Another mistake is that of joining a pronoun to the preceding word instead of the word following, thus: "If-I make." The natural joining here is "I-make" — not "if-I."

It is seldom advisable to phrase where the first word ends with a vowel or the second word begins with a vowel. Other examples of injudicious phrases are: "already-have," "and-when," "give-it," "credit-me," "far-more." The intervening vowel makes each of these forms appear as *one* word instead of a phrase-form. We said "seldom advisable," because there are some forms in which it is possible to join with safety and advantage — such forms as "very-many," "very-much," "very-great," "let-me," "tell-me," — but these are so common, so colloquial, that they have become familiar to the eye and mind. We think that although most writers join "very-many," "very-much," "very-great," few of them would join "very-well," simply because "well," being represented by a single stroke, is not sufficiently characteristic.

A careful study of the phrase-forms given in the Manual and Phrase Book will well repay the time so expended. These furnish types of phrases which if learned well will impress the idea upon the writer so that he can apply it to new phrases. — *Editorial in the* GREGG WRITER.

BUSINESS LETTERS

97. (46)

98. (55)

99. (56)

100. (66)

Dealers, generators, defective, replacements, we-have-drawn, balance, presentation, for-granted, next-ten-days, delayed, with-the-least-possible-delay, several-thousand, Northern-Pacific, specifications, dimensions, cut, tamarack, fir, pine, how-many, ties.

101. (67)

102. (71)

103. (74)

104.

Your-account, amounting, if-you-desire, to-take-advantage, it-will-be-necessary, to-send-us, we-ask-that, this-matter, early-attention, at-the-earliest-possible-moment, giving-this, personal-attention, my-letter, order-blank, price-list, instructions, this-claim, if-we-do-not, stockholders.

(76)

105.

(114)

106.

(115)

Relative, blocks, and-will-ship, uncompleted, at-as-early-a-date-as-possible, considerable, trouble, intentionally, preference, you-are-aware-of-the-fact, council, formal, proposed, paving, Massachusetts-Avenue, center-of-the, commissioners, greater-than, protests, calling-your-attention.

107.

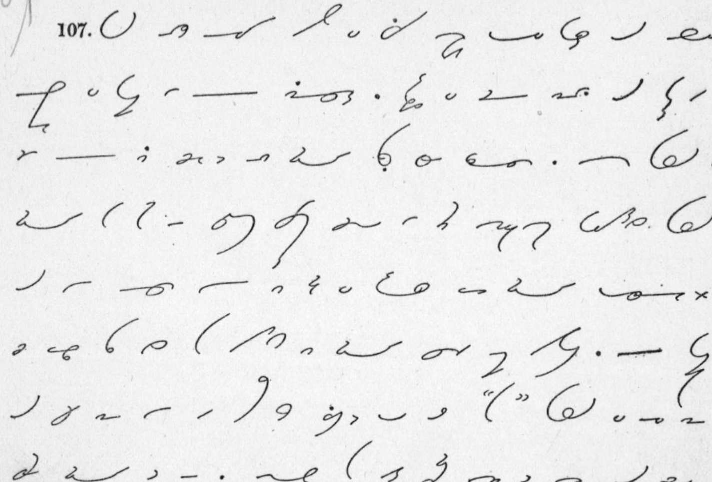

(218)

Competition, narrow, profit, specialty, wins, salt, buying, select, attractive, packages, co-operation, producing-that, source, honestly, profitable, heretofore, so-far-as, on-the-market, slip, sacks, branded, barrels, showing-this, guaranteed, in-the-market, and-let-us.

PIONEERS OF THE PACIFIC COAST

George H. Williams (175)

Slowly, wagons, dingy, oxen, travel-stained, depicted, anxious, abodes, discomforts, pioneers, wax, day-after-day, toilsome, resumed, Indian, scares, rugged, ascents, declivities, of-marvelous, beauty, gloomy, forests, majestic, mountains, genial, heavens.

SPEED STUDY XX

TWENTIETH LESSON

The "Jog." — Although it is of infrequent occurrence, the "jog" is important. Execute it as in "noun," "nounce," etc. Study and practice the following examples:

Key: renounce, announce, pronounce, denounce, pronoun, renown.

The "jog" in a few phrases in which it is applicable is also worthy of special practice.

Key: it-would, it-would-be, it-would-have, in-my, in-many.

The "jog" may be omitted in the following phrases:

Key: in-the-matter, on-the-matter, in-the-market, on-the-market.

Omission of Circle in "Earnest," etc. — When two circles are on the same side of a straight line, the line is liable in rapid writing to assume the appearance of a curve. For this reason the second circle is omitted in the word "earnest" to avoid conflict with the word "earliest."

Other examples are "hereinafter," (Compound Words, page 59 of the Manual), which is thus absolutely distinguished from "hereafter," and "agitate," "agitation." This also explains why the second circle in "lenient" is placed beneath the line.

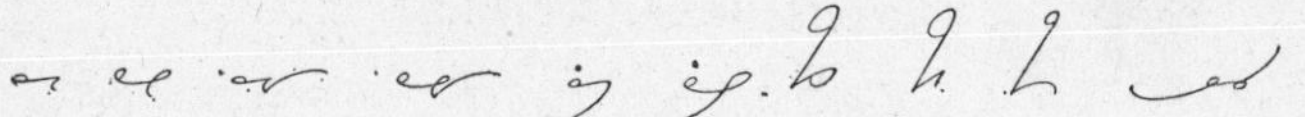

Key: earnest, earliest, earnest-attention, earliest-attention, hereinafter, hereafter, agitate, agitation, eject, lenient.

Mental Shorthand Practice.—There are many good ways of becoming familiar with the art when the student cannot conveniently write from dictation. He can read notes over and over again, which will strengthen his knowledge. He can, when listening to a speaker, mentally follow the words as they are uttered. If the student does not care to attempt to follow the speaker in that way, he may trace the outlines in the air, on his knee, on a sheet of paper, or on anything convenient, and it will be of benefit to him. Another good way is to take a newspaper, or any other printed work, and trace the shorthand characters with a lead pencil or pen directly over the printed words. — *Thomas P. Wilson.*

Enlarge Your Vocabulary by Reading. — The greatest trouble that employers find with average stenographers is that they have not enough general information. The ability to write shorthand at a moderate speed and to transcribe it on the typewriter should never be the ultimate goal of the ambitious stenographer. Improve yourself by reading, or better still, get some one to read good books to you on a variety of subjects so that you can take them down in shorthand. By this plan you fulfill a triple purpose. You improve your mind, enlarge your vocabulary, and add materially to your shorthand knowledge and speed. If you cannot get a fellow student to join you in this plan, you may be able to form a class of young people, who will meet once or twice a week or oftener and read aloud in turn. — *Frank Rutherford in* PRACTICAL POINTERS FOR SHORTHAND STUDENTS.

BUSINESS LETTERS

108. (74)

109. (96)

110.

Insurance-Company, that-they-are, suggestion, of-this-company, into-any, continental, that-comes, Minneapolis, Johnston, proof, under-policy, in-payment, the-reason, copy-of-the-form, in-these-cases, instead, Springfield, Walton, requests, to-delay, on-your-order, to-hold, specified, understood.

(91)

111.

(101)

112.

(107)

Urgently, of-these-goods, Danville, Davenport, Rockford, inasmuch-as, personally, Toledo, to-investigate, willingly, prosperous, between-us, Second-National-Bank, your-note, so-far-as-we-know, they-had, proceeds, so-long-a-time, elapsed, you-should-see, urgency, telling-you, we-need, badly.

113. (110)

114. (138)

Holmes, financially, indirectly, southern, California, New Jersey, Jersey City, Paterson, Newark, Trenton, Massachusetts, Boston, Worcester, Fall River, Lowell, Cambridge, Albany, Rochester, Buffalo, Baltimore, Richmond, to-New York, Philadelphia, Pittsburgh, Ohio, Pennsylvania.

115.

(241)

The-legal, description, southwest-quarter, township, range, east, Hanover, automobile, Phillips, choicest, state-of-Illinois, chocolate, loam, scattering, growth, hardwood, timber, neighborhood, prosperous, farmers, in-this-section, thirty-to-thirty-five-dollars, encumbered, on-or-before, equity.

THE REAL BUSINESSS MAN

William J. Bryan (202)

Definition, employer, attorney, corporation, counsel, metropolis, cross-roads, farmer, toils, summer, muscle, natural, resources-of-the-country, creates, Board-of-Trade, miners, a-thousand-feet, cliffs, hiding-places, precious, metals, poured, channels, financial, magnates, corner, deserving.

SPEED STUDY XXI

WORDSIGN DERIVATIVES

(1)

(2)

(3)

(4)

(5)

(6)

(7)

(8)

(9)

(10)

(11)

(12)

(13)

(14)

(15)

(16)

(17)

(18)

(19)

(20)

(21)

(22)

(23) (24)

(25)

(26)

(27)

(28) (29)

(30)

(31)

(32)

(33)

(34)

(35)

(36)

(37)

(38)

(39)

(40)

(41)

(42)

(43)

(44)

(45)

(46)

(47)

(48)

(49)

(50)

(51)

(52)

SPEED STUDY XXII

WORDSIGN DERIVATIVES — (Continued)

(53) (54) (55) (56) (57) (58) (59) (60) (61) (62) (63) (64) (65) (66) (67) (68) (69) (70)

(71) (72) (73) (74) (75) (76) (77) (78) (79) (80) (81) (82) (83)

KEY TO WORDSIGN DERIVATIVES

(To bring out the derivative suffixes and prefixes in the "Key" more clearly, the hyphen is used to express the root word.)

1. **Accept,** –s, –ed, –able, –ably, –ability, –or, –ation, un–able, non–ance.
2. **Accord,** –s, –ed, –ingly, –ant, –antly.
3. **Account,** –s, –ed, –able, –ably, –ability, –ant, –ancy, un–able, un–ability.
4. **Acknowledge,** –s, –ed, –ment, un–ed.
5. **Advantage,** –s, –ous, –ously, dis–, dis–s.
6. **Advertise,** –s, –ed, –ment, –er, –ers.
7. **Advise,** –s, –ed, –edly, –ability, –er, –ory, in–able, in–ability.

8. **Affect,** –s, –ed, –tion, –tionate, –tionately, –ation, –ive, dis–ed.
9. **Agree,** –s, –ed, –able, –ably, –ableness, –ability, –ment, dis–, dis–able.
10. **Allow,** –s, –ed, –able, –ance, un–able.
11. **Answer,** –s, –ed, –able, un–ed, un–able.
12. **Appoint,** –s, –ed, –able, –ee, –ment, –ive, dis–, re–.
13. **Avoid,** –s, –ed, –able, –ably, –ance, un–able.
14. **Beauty,** –ies, –eous, –eously, –iful, –ifully, –ify, –ifier.
15. **Bound,** –s, –ed, –less, –ary, a–, re–, un–ed.
16. **Capital,** –s, –ize, –ized, –ization, –ist, –ism, –ally, over–ize, over–ization.
17. **Care,** –s, –ed, –ful, –fully, –fulness, –less, –lessly, –lessness, over-ful.
18. **Change,** –s, –ed, –able, –ableness, –less, inter–, counter–.
19. **Character,** –s, –istic, –istically, –ize, –izes, –ization.
20. **Charge,** –s, –ed, –er, –able, dis–, over–, under–, re–, un–ed.
21. **Claim,** –s, –ed, –ant, –able, counter–, dis–, un–ed.
22. **Clear,** –s, –ed, –er, –est, –ness, –ance, –age, –cut.
23. **Client,** –s, –ele, –al, –age.
24. **Collect,** –s, –ed, –or, –orship, –tion, –ible, –ive, –ivity, –edly, un–ible.
25. **Consider,** –s, –ed, –ate, –able, –ably, in–ate, re–.
26. **Correct,** –s, –ed, –tion, –tional, –ly, –ness, –ive, in–, un–ed.
27. **Correspond,** –s, –ed, –ingly, –ent, –ents.
28. **Custom,** –s, –er, –ary, –arily, –house, ac–, unac–ed.
29. **Dear,** –s, –er, –ly, –est, –ness, en–, en–ingly.
30. **Deliver,** –s, –ed, –y, –er, –able, –ance.
31. **Desire,** –s, –ed, –able, –ability, –ous, un–able.
32. **Differ,** –s, –ed, –ently, –ential, –entiate, –entiation, in–ent, in–ently.
33. **Direct,** –s, –ed, –ly, –tion, –or, –orship, –ory, –orate, –ness, –ive, –orial, in–
34. **Effect,** –s, –ed, –ive, –ively, –iveness, –ual, –ually, –uality, in–ive, in–ual.
35. **Favor,** –s, –ed, –ite, –able, –ably, –itism, dis–, un–able.
36. **Firm,** –s, –ly, –er, –est, af–, con–.
37. **Form,** –s, –ed, –er, –erly, –al, –ulate.
38. **Give,** –s, –er, mis–ings, for–, unfor–n.
39. **Glad,** –ly, –dest, –ness, –den, –dened.
40. **God,** –s, –ly, –lier, –like, –less, –liness, –send, –speed, –father, –mother, un–ly.
41. **Good,** –ly, –y, –ness, –bye, –liness.
42. **Govern,** –s, –ed, –or, –orship, –able, –mental, –ess, mis–, un–able, ex–or.
43. **Great,** –er, –est, –ly, –ness.
44. **House,** –s, –ed, –ful, –hold, –holder, –keeping, –keeper, –wife, –work, ice–, ware–, ware-man.
45. **Industry,** –ies, –ious, –iously, –al, –alist, –alism.
46. **Kind,** –s, –est, –ness, –nesses, –ly, –liest, –liness, un–.

47. **Light,** –s, –ed, –er, –est, –ly, –en, –ening, –ened, –ness, a–, de–ful, en–en, en–enment, re–, un–ed.
48. **Like,** –s, –ed, –ly, –liness, –lihood, –en, –ness, –wise, –able, a–, dis–, un–ly.
49. **List,** –s, –ed, –less, –lessly, en–, en–ment, re-en–.
50. **Mail,** –s, –ed, –able, –ings, re–, un–able.
51. **Most,** –ly, fore–, in–, utter–, ut–, upper–.
52. **Move,** –s, –ed, –er, –able, –ie, –ment, re–, un–ed, im–able, counter–.
53. **Name,** –s, –ed, –ly, –less, mis–ed, un–ed, sur–, nick–.
54. **Object,** –s, –ed, –or, –tion, –tionable, –ive, –ively, un–tionable.
55. **Office,** –s, –er, –iate, –ious, –holder, inter–, sub–er.
56. **Official,** –s, –ism, –ly, un–.
57. **Popular,** –ly, –ity, –ize, –ization, un–.
58. **Power,** –s, –ful, –fully, –fulness, –less, em–, em–ed, over–.
59. **Purpose,** –s, –ly, –ful, –fully, –less, –lessness.
60. **Question,** –s, –ed, –er, –naire, –able, –ingly, un–able.
61. **Real,** –ly, –ism, –ist, –istically, –ity, –ty, –ize, –ization, un–.
62. **Receive,** –s, –ed, –er, –ership, –able, –ability, un–ed.
63. **Regard,** –s, –ed, –less, –ful, dis–, un–ed.
64. **Regret,** –s, –ed, –ful, –fulness, –able, –ably.
65. **Represent,** –s, –ed, –ative, –ation, mis–ation, un–ed.
66. **Respect,** –s, –ed, –er, –able, –ability, –ive, –fulness, dis–.
67. **Speak–speech,** –s, –er, –ership, –able, –less, –lessness, –maker, be–.
68. **Spirit,** –s, –ed, –less, –ual, –uality, –ualist –ualistic, –uous, dis–ed.
69. **State,** –s, –ed, –ly, –liness, –ment, –sman, –smanship, –smanlike, –hood, mis–ment.
70. **Stock,** –s, –ed, –holder, –y, –ily, –ings.
71. **Success,** –es, –or, –ful, –fully, –sion, –ive, –ively, un–ful.
72. **System,** –s, –atize, –atized, –atizer, –atization, –atic, –atically, un–atic.
73. **Thank,** –s, –ed, –ful, –fully, –fulness, –less, –lessness, –sgiving, un–ful.
74. **Trust,** –s, –ed, –ingly, –ee, –eeship, –ful, –worthy, dis–, mis–, anti–, in–, un–worthy.
75. **Truth,** –s, –ful, –fully, –fulness, –less, un–.
76. **Use,** –s, –ed, –ful, –less, –able, –er, –age, –ance, un–ed, mis–, dis–.
77. **Value,** –s, –ed, –ation, –able, –less, over–, under–.
78. **Week–weak,** –s, –ly, –ness, –en, –ened, bi–ly.
79. **Wire,** –s, –ed, –y, –iness, –less.
80. **Wonder,** –s, –ed, –ful, –fully, –ment, –ingly.
81. **Work,** –s, –ed, –er, –ings, –able, –man, –manship, –manlike, –house, over–.
82. **World,** –s, –ly, –liness, un–ly.
83. **Write–right,** –s, –ed, –er, –ings, –ful, –fully, –ly, up–, down–, a–.

BUSINESS LETTERS

116.

(150)

117.

Henry, Seymour, Kansas-City, exposure, weather, conditions, built, start, finish, protected, paint, iron, wood, decay, found, Union, county, building, repairing-the, let-us, save, will-find, savings, Saginaw, Michigan, bankers, no-doubt, chances, good-many, loans, farms.

(130)

118.

(136)

Locality, vicinity, issued, quarter, interested, mutually, fiscal, March, favorably, Adam, Bowman, Memphis-Tennessee, your-order, rather-than, selected, costs, regularly, sells, fault, extra, if-you-find, for-any-reason, at-our-expense, we-thank-you-for-the-order.

119. (160)

120.

Mortgage-Company, Salem, if-you-can-see, to-increase, continual, ever-since, barn, under-construction, drill, we-desire, to-whom, security, of-improving, real-estate, investment, Fred, Churchill, Omaha, Nebraska, probability, fact-that-the, coffee, will-advance, sight, how-much.

(131)

121.

(157)

Noticed, hesitate, to-guarantee, decline, Armstrong, Akron, Model, Wright, biplane, machines, rebuilding, exhibition, I-should-like-to-know, to-sell, propeller, brackets, shafts, chains, I-should, horse-power, outfit, would-not-have, purposes, museum, procure, photograph, I-took, hydroplane.

122.

(154)

123.

Pollard, Hartford, shrapnel, Delaware, Locomotive, loading-the, shells. property, in-this-state, becoming, figure, we-want, to-tell-us, early-reply, MacIntosh, Wheeling, West-Virginia, folder, Lily, Evaporated, Milk, process, grocery-department, familiarize, essential.

(128)

124.

(143)

Food-department, dry, clothing, folders, International, Motor-Company, Troy, cylinder, gas, engine, feature, capable, soil, mainly, volcanic, combined, harvester, necessarily, pressure, steep, rough, weight, as-light-as-possible, yet, we-do-not-want, endeavoring, low-priced.

125.

(125)

126.

Slater, El-Paso, Texas, six-per-cent, gold, denominations, earnings, children, grows, in-the-course-of-a-few-years, we-shall-be-glad-to-receive, to-reserve, Theodore, Butler, Des-Moines, Iowa, American, Surety-Company, Harvey, McKinnon, Burlington, ditch, contract, authority, attached.

(142)

127.

(129)

128

Printed, of-such, acknowledgment, and-I-am-writing-you, Horace, Arnold, Green-Bay, Wisconsin, deeds, described, offered, accurate, reliable, properties, sufficiently, reporting-the, moral, risk, each-case, as-soon-as-possible, Laura, Henderson, Duluth, Minnesota, My-dear-Miss.

(131)

129.

Enter-the, Senior, entrance, ideal, Art, Institute, libraries, numerous, bathing, beaches, play-grounds, park, recreational, extensive, equipment, enrollment, illustrated, Ernest, Tracy, Leavenworth, Kansas, newest, features, accordingly, instructing, Stewart, South-Avenue, Topeka.

(167)

130.

(133)

Interesting, visit, profitable, in-the-meantime, perhaps, lend, Bureau, maintained, special, we-invite, cordially, Arthur, Herrick, Seattle, Washington, advising-me, from-my, membership, six-hundred, including, mercantile, Curtis, round-table, luncheons, of-them, sincere, belief.

GETTYSBURG ADDRESS

Score, years-ago, fathers, continent, conceived, liberty, dedicated, all-men, created, equal, engaged, civil, whether-that, nation, endure, battle-field, we-have-come, portion, their-lives, fitting, proper, we-should, larger, consecrate, hallow, power, detract, forget, unfinished, fought.

Abraham Lincoln **(268)**

SELF-READING SHORTHAND

Task, honored, increased, devotion, they-gave, measure, highly, resolve, shall-not-have, died, in-vain, under-God, freedom, for-the-people, perish, earth, prophets, spelled, dictation, and-lose, won't, illegible, outline, speed, angels, symbols.

W. E. McDermut (260)

THE GENIUS OF PERSISTENCE

Faster, on-the-other-hand, speed, imaginative, critical, faculties, faults, in-the-course-of-time, acquire, to-coin, self-reading, jump, of-their-own, notebook, young-men, practical, virtue, persistence, candidates, burden, climber, must-have, subway, ground.

Push, climbing, legs, gained, reach, height, Faraday, scientist, dropped, tiny, screw, twilight, assistant, consequence, defeated, habit, succeed, must-become, shining, thread, that-must-be, woven, character, scarlet, rope, jeweled, brightest, outlook, upon-life, patient, plodders.

Newell Dwight Hillis (297)

PRODUCTIVE EMPLOYMENT

Mark, Hopkins, brilliant, carried, recitations, don't-be, afraid, doubt, talents, possess, literally, robs, mental, development, individuality, imitation, someone-else, roads, choose, neighbor, if-you-get, to-start, journey, hide, under-a-bushel, burning, to-grow, feed, fire, feeble, flame, besides.

William A. Field (299)

EARNESTNESS

Alexanders, conquer, worlds, equally, sight-of-the-fact-that-the, happiness, associated, naturally, darkness, just, so-much-as, productive, extent, surroundings, less-than, unyielding, lavishes, contentment, on-him, who-finds, vigorous, prosecution, untiring, attribute, commanded, earnestness.

Lord Lytton (226)

LIBERTY AND UNION

Afford, establish, foot, solid, gradual, onward, sudden, over-a, precipice, maxims, deduce, caution, resists, temptation, implies, inviolable, in-the-world, implicitly, frequently, preferred, applicants, lifts, station, reputation, accustomed, hang, disunion, short-sight, fathom, below.

Counsellor, preserved, tolerable, destroyed, lasts, exciting, gratifying, prospects, to-penetrate, veil, on-my, opened, behind, eyes, to-behold, dishonored, fragments, glorious, dissevered, discordant, belligerent, drenched, fraternal, blood, lingering, gorgeous, trophies, luster, polluted, obscured.

Daniel Webster **(308)**

THE GREATER THRIFT

Motto, no-such, miserable, interrogatory, delusion, folly, afterwards, over-in, of-living, blazing, over-the-land, wind, under-the-whole, sentiment, forever, inseparable, misunderstanding, scope, lies, primarily, striving, differentiate, practice, reminded, who-said, whether, speculative, mixed.

S. W. Straus (298)

Declared, of-wealth, of-mental, foundation, of-all, honor, individual, through-its, chasm, thrift, stones, no-more, house, detriment, thrifty, consists, judicious, physical, merely, we-have-gone, undesirable, of-misers, wheels, turned, men-and-women, sanely, money-saving, link, strand.

SPEED STUDY XXIII

SIMILAR WORDS

	adapt		attainment		causation
	adopt		atonement		concession
	admonish		borough		cessation
	admonition		bureau		secession
	ammunition		brown		cities
	adverse		burn		citizen
	averse		burned		citizenship
	affect		burnt		civil
	effect		can't		several
	agriculture		count		claims
	agricultural		cares		class
	annual		case		clients
	annul		carton		collation
	appear		cartoon		collision
	happen		curtain		collusion, collection

command	decease	discussion
commend	disease	dissection
comment	desist	destination
common	dedication	distance
commerce	deduction	distant
commercial	detection	destined
commission	decent, dissent	distinct
company, keep	descend	distinguished
complain, complete	descent	desirability
creditable	defect	disturb
credible	difficulty	earliest
damnation	defy	earnest
domination	deify	election, elusion
denomination	divide	elision
debtor	diligence	illusion
deter	diligent	allusion

electric	expansive	hereafter
electrical	expensive	hereinafter
embarrass	extant	high
embrace	extent	highly
England	fault	human
English	fought	humane
envious	fort	impassioned
invoice	fellows	impatient
esteem	philosophy	imperil
estimate	philosopher	imperial
except	fortune	inattention
expect	fourteen	intention
excess	finish	indulge
exist	furnish	indulgent
expand	garden	ingenious
expend	guardian	ingenuous

BUSINESS LETTERS

131.

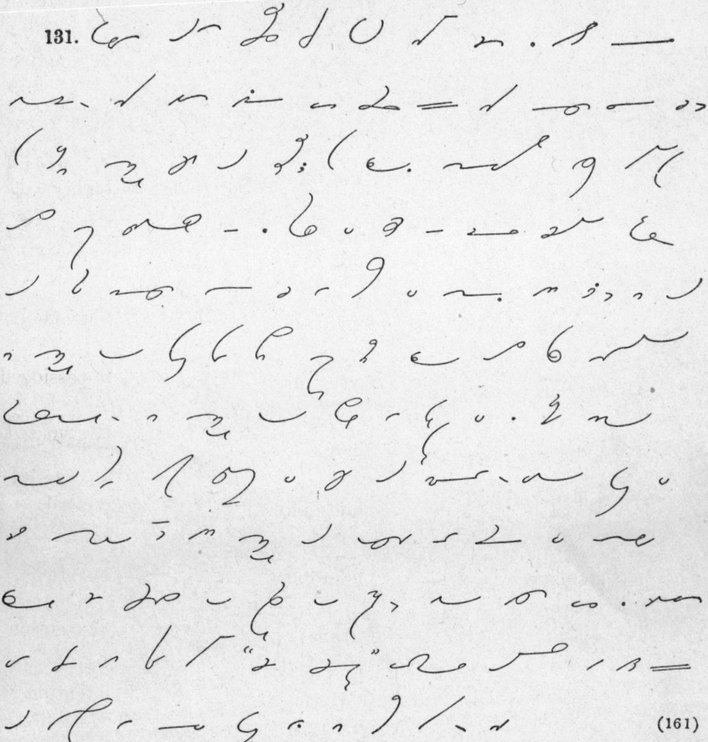

(161)

132.

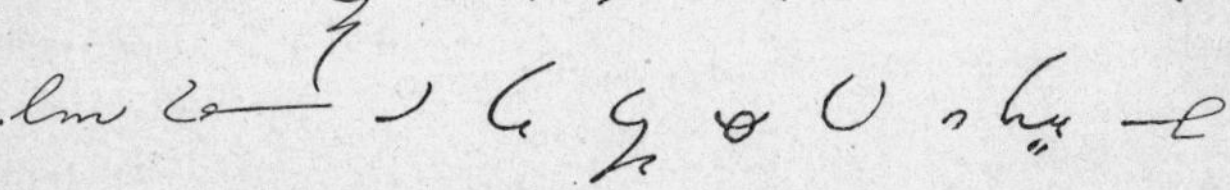

Savannah, deaf, offering-your, commodities, durability, utilized, variety, ways, spring, combination, flannels, possibilities, soft, wool, cloth, double, attractiveness, warmth, react, fabrics, washable, stroke, jot, down, Freeman, Brothers, Providence, Rhode-Island, Burroughs.

(193)

133.

Trade, exchange, that-date, machine, there-would-be, that-could, few-years, remarkable, developments, you-could, event, models, over-and, fill, and-return, give-you, including-the, Herman, Stebbins, Indianapolis, you-asked, samples, chinchilla, cloakings.

(173)

134.

Dropping-you, reminder, they-want, if-they-have, widely, easily, just-as-well, seasonable, year, preparedness, watchword, demand, end-of-the-season, available, Whitney, Jacksonville, Florida, advertisements, high-priced, cuts, store, free-of-charge, you-find.

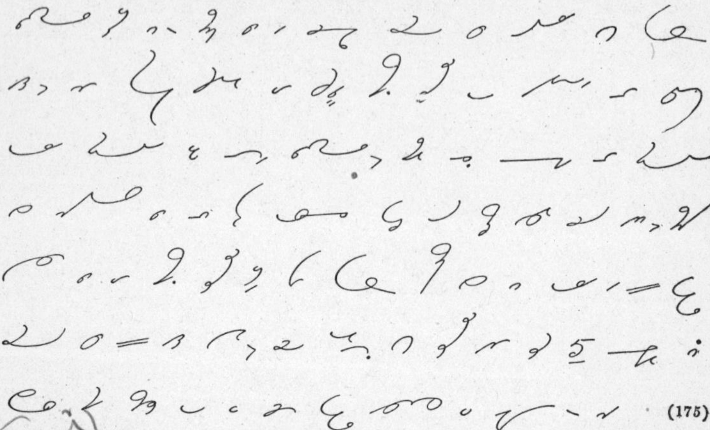

(175)

135.

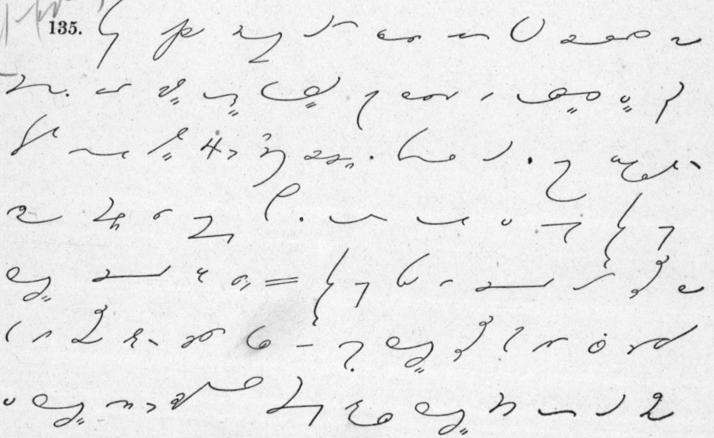

With-this-letter, offers, simply, Fayette, I-shall-see, I-suggest, filled, restricting, apply, as-these, take-care, at-the-present-time, Benjamin, Sullivan, Syracuse, we-learn-that, figuring, water, erected, Lima, Ohio, bids, cement, pride (private), Alpha.

(188)

136.—

Bidder, either, Drake, Consumers, Fuel, Supply-Company, very-glad, you-write-us, Wilcox, Portland, few-weeks-ago, subscription, entered, Magazine, reader, we-feel-sure-that, each-number, inspiration, beneficial, perfecting-your, remodeling, problem, exterior, design, fulfill, architects.

(204)

137.

Contains, Scott's, publications, privileged, information-department, experience, yours-very-cordially, Lewis, Turner, Salt-Lake-City, Utah, realizes, looks, around, observes, wastes, greater-than, accumulations, equivalent, conservative, American-people, investor, one-thousand-dollars, secured.

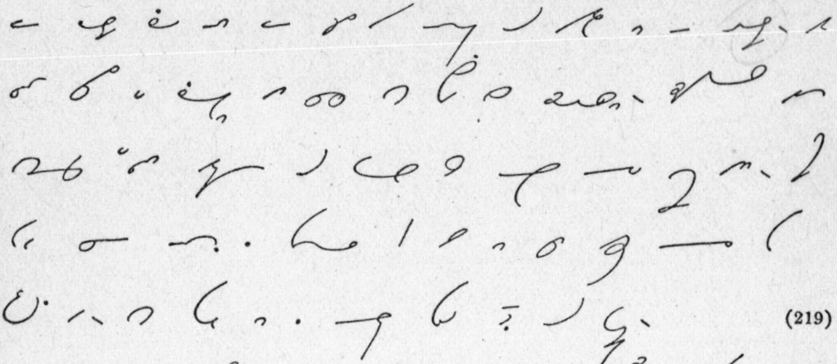

(219)

138.—

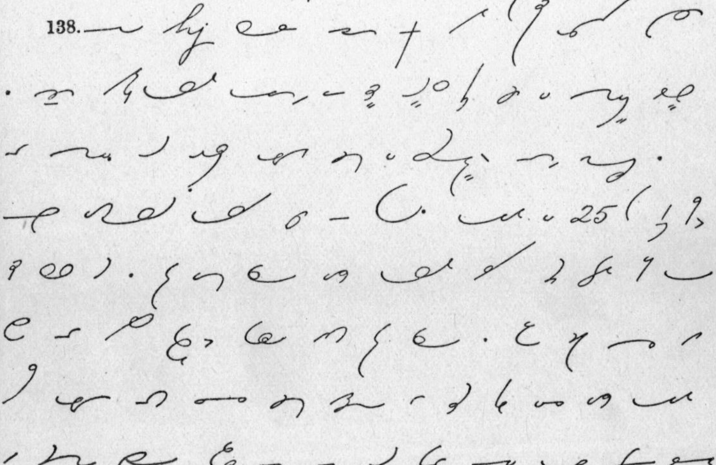

Encourage, discipline, helping-you, over-with-you, at-such-time, to-save, message, Allen, retained, quick, disposition-of-the-lands, End-Avenue, Grove, growing, thriving, residential, Valesburg, of-this-land, one-hundred-feet, prior, to-secure, figures.

(200)

139.

Sacrifice, owner, realizing-that, will-give, and-mail, 9-a.-m., 6-p.-m., at-our-offices, room, Comstock, await, Brake-Company, to-produce, sending-these, we-have-taken, Printers', results, names, circularizing, superintendent, strengthen, campaign, agree-with-us.

(166)

140.—16 ... 25 ...

Oscar, Stevens, Bronxville, dumped, passengers, short-haul, has-never, largely, tributary, controversy, precipitated, causes, doubtless, diminishing, from-month-to-month, from-year-to-year, comfortable, abnormal, traffic exorbitant, at-the-present-moment, electric-engines, Electric-Zone.

(201)

141.—

(197)

Tend, Baldwin, St.-Paul, Attorney-General, Atwood, nominated, sheriff, primary, election, resided, many-years, naturalized, of-this-country, nomination, filed, petition, citizenship, under-such, in-my-opinion, eligible, elector, constitutional, statutory, provision, assuming-that.

GREAT ART

Expression-of-the-mind, foolishly, sensibly, virtuous, vicious, basely, thoughtful, honest, cemented, if-it-has, ornament, carver, greedy, insensitive, stupid, buildings, microscope, magnified, a-hundred-fold, passionate, intensifies, noblest, meanest, delights, under-a, scalpel dissection, misrepresent.

John Ruskin (313)

A MAN PASSES FOR THAT HE IS WORTH

Inmost, likes, imagination, affections, perseverance, impatience, clumsiness, cleverness, cobweb, it-was-made, spider, honeycomb, cast, worm, nest, wreathed, bird, worthily, ignobly, least, idle, curiosity, peoples', estimate, of-remaining, unknown, pledge, assembly, enters, attempts.

Gauged, stamped, troop, whoop, square, newcomer, accurately, weighed, undergone, stranger, distant, trinkets, pockets, pretentions, sniffs, divine, searches, transpierces, distinguished, Homer, feigned, Iliad, drove, Xerxes, christianized, abolished, slavery, reverence, commands, devils.

Ralph Waldo Emerson (332)

FAMOUS WOMEN WORKERS

18

Utterly, magnanimity, greets, unexpectedly, helpful, obliged, by-means, daily, faithfully, skillfully, ample, biography, to-honor, of-others, talent, thus, great-numbers, indefatigable, musicians, artists, authors, scientists, splendid, achievements, among, Rosa, Bonheur, favorite. animal, steadily.

Vocations for Girls (327)

Louisa, Alcott, ceaselessly, Larcom, poems, operative, Kate, Douglas, Wiggin, enthusiastic, teacher, charming, stories, Clara, Barton, founder, Florence, Nightingale, unlimited, to-promote, wonderful, abilities, deficiency.

TENACITY OF ATTENTION

Tenacious, strongest, factors, cultivated, psychologists, hardly, overestimate, of-some, geniuses, accomplishes, undivided, they-might-have half-the-time, scorned, restraint, butterfly, element, demanded, meadow, flowers, quicker, watch, ant's, latter, winter, surpass, tortoise, beat.

Reuben Post Halleck (328)

THE BASIS OF SPEED

Happened, no-matter, quickly, that-might-be, succeeded, something-else, the-only-way, to-cultivate, continuous, wanders, consecutive, powers, each-time, weariness, colt, one-side-of-the-street, anywhere, pulled, understanding, particular, fundamental, mastered, attainment, incomplete.

Royal, dogged, if-you-do-not, textbook, once-in-a-while, feel-sure-that, perfectly, under-control, fixed, in-your-mind, wordsigns, contractions, outlines, briefer, of-legibility, groundwork, you-are-in-a-position, stenographer, procrastinators, seldom, nervous, energy, direction, intelligent, acquisition.

Willard B. Bottome (327)

THE FUNCTION OF LITERATURE

Systematic, pianist, prima, donna, walk, upright, do-not, accidental, who-wrote, effluence, core, served, translated, actual, it-does-not, vehicle, reason, instinct, powerful, in-this, battle, reservoir, emotions, constituted, deprived, intellect, activity, exceptionally.

Arnold Bennett (326)

Retract, to-disappear, accessible, storage, correspondingly, degraded, fallacious, petty, upward, pull, conceiving, realized, function, exists, the-living, essence, minor, agreeable, harmless, fashion, momentary, faint, multitudes, habitual, readers, utilize, implication, golf, soporifics, devices.

SPEED STUDY XXIV

SIMILAR WORDS — (Continued)

inside
insight
instant
instantaneous
intelligent
intelligence
indent
intend
into
unto
invest
investigate
labors
laborious
lawyer
lower

libel
liable
likable
looks
luxury
man
men
matter
mature
memoranda
memorandum
mention
mission
motion
negligence
neglect

operation
oppression
ordain
ordinary
ours, hours
recent
parcel
partial
partition
petition
passionate
patient
permanent
prominent
persecute
prosecute

persecution
prosecution
poor
power
pure
praised
pressed
presented
probation
prohibition
reassume
resume

remark
remember, remain
remit
revel
reveal
reverence
revere
series
serious
signal
signature
significant

special
specify
specific
sport
support
circuit
starred
started
succeed
success
woman
women

"Pre" and "Pro" Prefixes.—"Pre" is always written in full, except in "presume" and its derivatives.

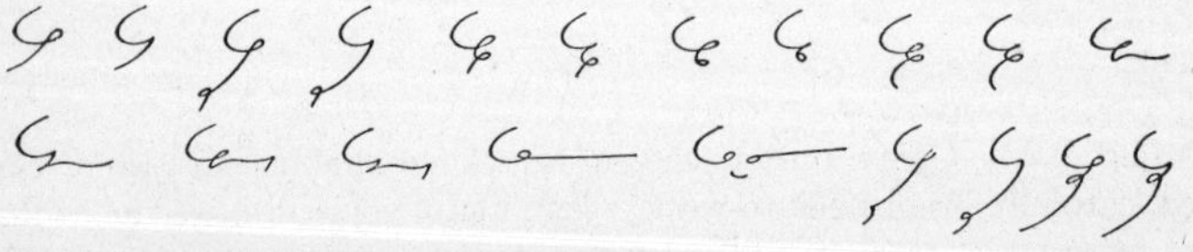

Key: prefer, perfect, prevision, provision, precision, procession, precede, proceed, precept, percept, prescribe, proscribe, prescription, proscription, premium, pre-eminent, previous, perverse, preserve, persevere.

BUSINESS LETTERS

142.—

(199)

143.—

Cutler, Battle-Creek, butter, cheese, eggs, level, at-the-same-time, curtailed, carefully, from-week-to-week, accumulate, you-will-have, following-these, very-large, extra-profit, so-long-as, to-do, to-convert, as-rapidly-as-possible, that-this-is, active, handling, sales, Alvin, Steele, Brooklyn.

(174)

144.

Manor, the-house, advertised, has-since, however, desirable, cellar, dwelling, baths, parlor, veranda, porch, electric-light, beautiful, Long-Island, Neck, Hills, to-settle, bargain, investigate, we-shall-be, to-inspect, at-your-convenience, Nash, Newburgh, Boys'-Department, branch, Y. M. C. A.

(211)

145.

Quarters, older, and-has, needed, furniture, to-replace, other-days, generously, donations, I-am-sure-that-the, of-these-days, appeals, to-show, in-raising-the, good-deal, spent, we-count, I-shall, Waldron, Huntington, short-time-ago, article, explaining, cent.

(179)

146.

Forced, economize, relax, expenses, absorb, merchant, prosperity, progressive, taking-advantage, that-may-be, feeling-that, you-have-taken, worry, Pearce, Montreal, Quebec, slogan, Canadian, manufacturer, laborer, Canada, varieties, which-are-not, United States, logical.

(168)

147.—

Dealer, take-advantage, superior, we-can-give-you, you-want, Willard, O'Donnell, Holyoke, we-thank-you-for-your-inquiry, every-case, we-have-no, to-submit, to-you, as-to-your, decease, we-shall-be-able, this-company, executor, trusts, thereby, entitled, trust-company, suggestive.

(177)

148.

We-hope, further, strictly, confidential, Robbins, Webster, Council-Bluffs, illustrations, pages, output, attach, regular, switch, insulating, accompanying, blue-print, circuit, screws, short-lines, furnished, upon-request, Republic.

(198)

149.

Obligation, Putnam, New-Haven, my-attention-to-the-fact, I-wish-to-make, particularly, desirous, agencies, city, thoroughfares, practically, population, suburbs, effectively, economically, bulletins, continuously, advertiser, to-convince, painted, as-they-were.

(210)

150.

Within-our, Moody, New-Orleans, soap, expect, improvement, fact-that, justify, tonnage, assortment, justifies, outlets, recognized, if-anything, to-forge, strides, to-a-large-extent, pushing-this, commodity, forthcoming, salesmen, to-understand, on-which-they-are.

(203)

151.

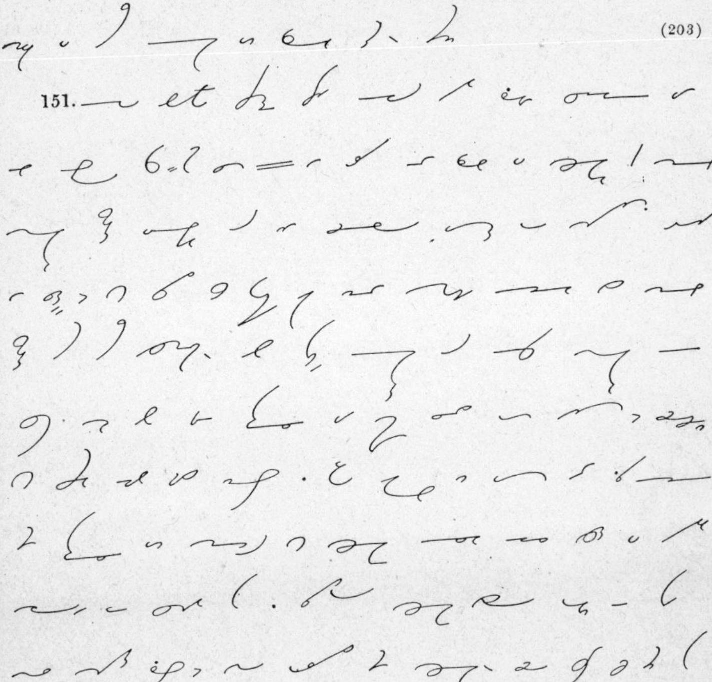

Co-operation, very-cordially yours, Jackson, Butte, Montana, announcement, national, pay-up, campaigns, clubs, conducting, movements, boosted, memberships, can-be-done, educational, that-will, hereafter, paving-the, sending-the, prospective.

(195)

152.

(192)

Mayor, involves, demonstration, neighborly, community's, generosity, kindliest, to-surrender, cheerful, compliance, facilitate, initiate, authorities, five-hundred-thousand, consolidation, industrial, perplexing, obstacle, deserved, recognition, cordial, suggesting-this, obvious, solution.

TURNING THE GRINDSTONE

When-I-was, winter's, accosted, smiling, axe, shoulder, grindstone, yes-sir, compliment, patting, how-could, refuse, kettle, what's, your-name, waiting, reply, I-am-sure, finest, few-minutes, tickled, flattery, fool, toiled, tugged, till, tired, to-death, bell, blistered.

Benjamin Franklin (359)

COUNTING THE COST

Sharpened, rascal, you've, truant, scud, to-school, you'll, alas, grindstone, too-much, sank, in-my-mind, over-polite, to-grind, flattering-the, professions, attachment, who-is, private, tyrant, me-thinks, hoisted, qualification, to-render, respectable, doomed, booby, if-it-were-not, who-would.

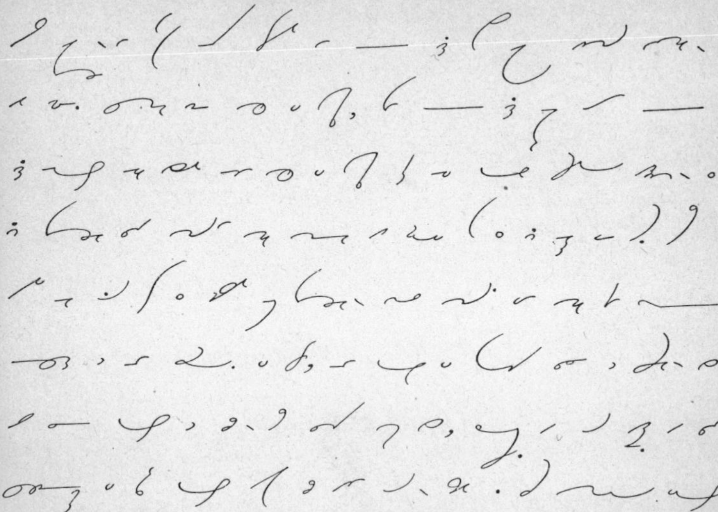

Parable, to-count, the-cost, warning, fatal, to-success, counting-the, sorrow, insists, starts, the-real, elevating, accumulations, toughening, as-it-is, to-faint, of-us, weary, discouraged, struggles, wisdom, which-have, to-ourselves, to-do-it, before-night.

Phillips Brooks (355)

PLAYING THE GAME

No-man, wished, it-would-have, exhilaration, untrodden, Columbus, the-whole, before, have-been, every-man, who-did-not, somehow, this-thing, which-we-are, search, everybody, loves, pretty, everyone, as-well-as, every-other, person, excel, football, baseball, physically, unfitted, outclass.

Wilfred T. Grenfell (347)

Do-not-think, rooter, value, of-life, genius, do-not-be, discouraged, of-themselves, few-years, brilliantly, clever, workers, who-have-given, prizes, measured, will-never, rightly, despises, quitter, I'm-not, cares, winner, walk-over, anyhow, to-fight, for-yourself, things.

FREE EDUCATION

Repeatedly, comprising, treasure, thief, misfortune, poverty, safer-than, shelter, thrilled, realization, the-word, we-understood, who-had, who-could-not, pronounce, who-was-not, rulings, exclusions, the-doors, stood, the-way, incident, impressed, to-experience, disappointment.

Mary Antin (372)

SUCCESS IN SHORTHAND

Father, enter-upon-our, he-said, that-the-time, interval, crowded, to-visit, dressed, to-learn-the, mysteries, washboard, speaking-tube, to-trade, pedler, window, policeman, English, assisted, gallery, to-become, intelligently, applied, depends, you-must-have, ambition.

Shorthand, bread-winning, accomplishment, pronunciation, language, immense, disciplines, analyze, constructive, sharpens, unequaled, one-of-the-most, young-woman, expert, of-all-these, expertness, brevity, uniformity, proportion, observed, distinguish, positively, strokes, obtained.

The Gregg Writer (349)

STENOGRAPHY A FERTILE FIELD

Execution, characters, facility, even-the, practicing-the, alphabet, acquired, stenography, fertile, great, successes, comparatively, nearly, competent, privilege, elbow, trained, positions, in-itself, forceful, personalities, fingers, wide-awake, closer.

Edward J. Kilduff (365)

Valuable, bits, of-information, customs, transactions, moreover, stimulus, is-at-hand, stenographer, direct, advancement, into-the, career, secretary, realize, he-should, alive, wide-awake, competency, hidden, in-any-other, since-the, to-display, promotion.

SPEED STUDY XXV

NAMES OF WOMEN

Key: (1) Adeline, Agnes, Alice, Alma, Amanda, Amelia, Annabelle, Antoinette, (2) Augusta, Barbara, Beatrice, Belle, Bertha, Blanche, Bridget, Caroline, Catherine, (3) Celia, Charlotte, Clara, Constance, Cora, Cynthia, Delia, Dorothy, Edith, (4) Edna, Eleanor, Elizabeth, Eliza, Emily, Emma, Esther, Ethel, Flora, (5) Florence, Frances, Georgiana, Gertrude, Grace, Hannah, Harriet, Helen, Henrietta, (6) Hortense, Ida, Irene, Isabelle, Jean, Jeanette, Josephine, Judith, Julia, Juliet, Laura, (7) Lillian, Louise, Lucy, Mabel, Margaret, Maria, Marian, (8) Marie, Mary, Martha, Matilda, Mildred, Nancy, Norah, (9) Olive, Ophelia, Pauline, Pearl, Phyllis, Phoebe, Priscilla, Prudence, Rachel, (10) Rebecca, Rosalie, Ruth, Sarah, Sophia, Stella, Susan, Sylvia, Victoria, Violet.

NAMES OF MEN

1

2

3

4

5

6

7

8

9

10

Key: (1) Abraham, Adam, Adolph, Albert, Alex, Alfred, Andrew, Anthony, Arthur, (2) Benjamin, Charles, Clarence, Daniel, David, Donald, Duncan, Edgar, (3) Edmond, Edward, Edwin, Ernest, Eugene, Felix, Francis, Frank, Frederick, Geoffrey, (4) George, Gilbert, Godfrey, Guy, Harold, Henry, Herbert, Hiram, Hubert, (5) Hugh, Hugo, Isaac, Jacob, James, Jesse, Joel, John, Jonathan, Joseph, Joshua, Josiah, (6) Julian, Lawrence, Leonard, Louis, Mark, Martin, Matthew, Morris, (7) Michael, Moses, Nathan, Nathaniel, Nicholas, Norman, Oliver, (8) Oscar, Owen, Patrick, Paul, Peter, Philip, Ralph, Raymond, Richard, (9) Robert, Roger, Rudolph, Rufus, Rupert, Samuel, Simon, Solomon, (10) Stephen, Theodore, Thomas, Timothy, Victor, Vincent, Vivian, Walter, William.

BUSINESS LETTERS

153.

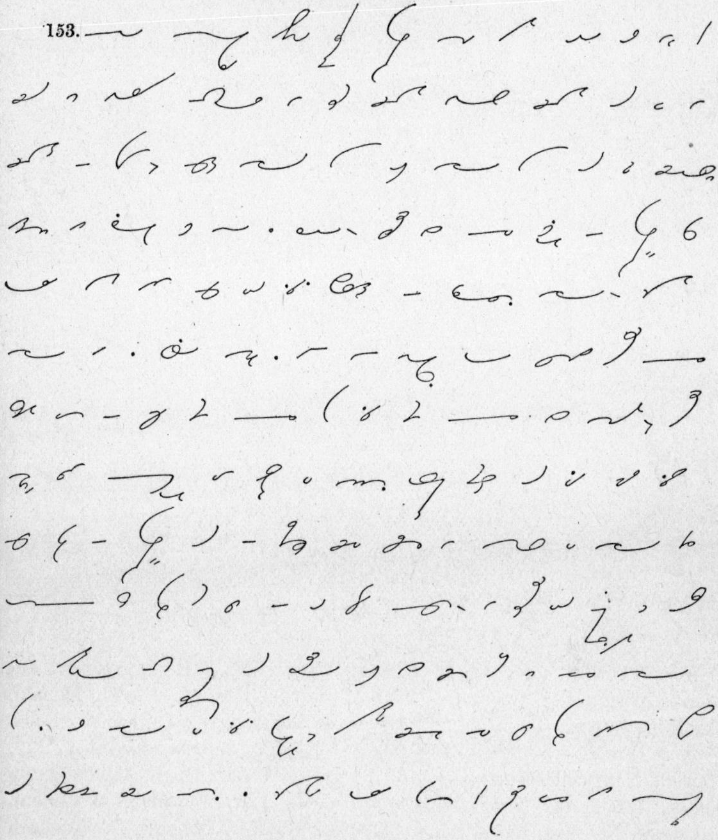

Gilbert, Jefferson, Bridgeport, Connecticut, sentences, to-ask-you, householders, heating, apparatus, coal, sometimes, higher, ton, counts, consulted, types, cooking, furnaces, hot, heaters, exactly, recommend, engineering-departments, entirely, disposal, to-do-so, postal-card.

(228)

154.

Number, Messrs., Thompson, Birmingham, Alabama, calling-your-attention, defects, as-follows, ashes, wooden, supposed, receptacles, doors, recoated, tin, metal, worn, closed, removal, overhauled, crack, opening, heat, basement, oily, waste, provided, concrete, brick, laid, protective, inches.

(227)

155.

Sides-of-the-range, noncombustible, so-as-to, preclude, possibility, sparks, fat, boiling-over, Leonard, Monroe, Oklahoma, probably, wasted, we-did-not, spare,. if-we-had, saved, ourselves, much-time, escaped, discouragements, disappointments, he-realizes, to-impress, upon-such, self-training.

(247)

156.

We-ask-you, to-co-operate, you-would-like-to-see, scholarship, transfer, holder, to-choose, Tyler, Joplin, in-answer-to-your-letter, alternating, to-making-you, central, stations, equipped, to-such-an-extent, overstocked, with-them, and-have.

(223)

157.—

Sort, endeavor, to-dispose, frankly, Elbert, Gibson, Utica, as-requested, self-balancing, sportsmen, seaplane, over-any-other, existing, manifold, on-account-of-the-fact, operator, reduced, one-half, enabling, to-fly, perform, propellers, arc, unprecedented, seaworthy, sustained.

(222)

158.

Pontoon, balanced, wing, center-of, gravity, enabled, under-more, unsatisfactory, airplane, tanks, diagrams, thank-you-for-your-inquiry, Grand-Rapids, widespread, Packard, product, rumors, afloat, voluntary, options, Detroit, for-example, to-date, suggest-that, whose, you-would-like-to-have.

(234)

159.

Unheard-of, prediction, freely, premiums, convention, we-found, groups, estimate, each-one-of-our, invitation, announcement, Dearborn, Racine, asphalt, shingle, in-mind, summer, as-well-as-the, cold, was-not, materials, over-half, century's.

(255)

160.

Ingenuity, modern, melting, it-would-not, varying, temperatures, year-after-year, samples, colors, having-been, guarantee, backed, Roofing, Registration, uniform, idea-of-the-types, Shandler, Plainfield, Judson, University, permission, organizing.

(255)

161.

Aviation, corps, alumni, observers, pilots, arises, seven-or-eight, high-speed, scout, heavier, hydro-aeroplane, want-to-make, three-or-four, maintenance, at-your-earliest-convenience, descriptive, full-information, inquiries, prominence, it-might-be, notoriety, Oliver, Perkins, Chattanooga.

(210)

Associations, retail, wholesale, clubs, boards-of-trade, seems-to-me, wise, to-furnish, comprehensive, Government, for-the-purpose, unifying, accounting, bookkeeping, standardizing, approval, in-addition-to-the, federal, commission, industries, coöperate, parties, remedy, solved.

ASSOCIATION AND MEMORY

Retains, associates, hangs, to-fish, sunk, beneath-the, surface, network, attachments, tissue, secret, diverse, multiple, to-retain, as-much-as-possible, outward, native, tenacity, who-thinks, over-his, weaves, relations, each-other, examples, their-own, college, athlete, dunce, astonish.

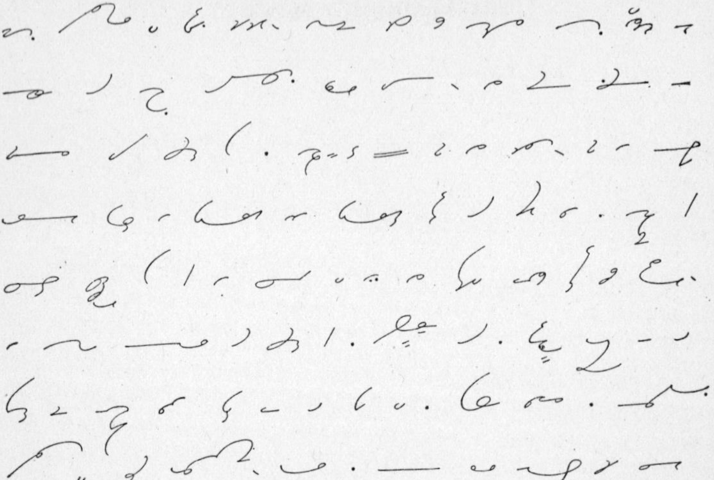

William James (390)

Dictionary, sporting, over-these-things, concept-system, politician, votes, copiousness, amazes, outsiders, bestow, Darwin, Spencer, incompatible, middling, physiological, retentiveness, verifying, theory, cluster, cling, grapes, stem, discern, erudition, desultory, unutilizable, unnoted.

THE BUSINESS CAREER

Conducted, smallest, scale, occupied, indeed, enterprise, gigantic, partners, huge, rulers, domain, confidently, career, abundant, exercise, of-man's, highest, human-nature, captain, favorable, ripening, prejudice, I-do-know, permanent, obtainable, honorable, irreproachable.

Judgment, human-life, foolish, irregular, suspected, sharp, profession, child, beyond-the, all-round, stern, supreme, reward, yields, benefactions, universities, educational, institutions, Girard, Lehigh, Chicago, Harvard, Yale, Cornell, to-succeeding, generations, hallowed, blessings, thousands.

Andrew Carnegie **(392)**

IMAGINATION IN BUSINESS

Sound, liberal, Napoleon, dead, soldiers, inscribed, Pompey's, Pillar, rules, morals, in-part, absolutely, devoid, emotion, one-thing, namely, the world's, inventions, watched, scuffling, stubbing, meant, copper, across-the, a-million-dollars.

Lorin F. Deland (395)

Millions, aside, waterfall, Niagara, electric-lamps, city-of-Buffalo, confining, the-workings, arts, applicable, and-with-the, exception, concisely, synthesis, analysis, of-things, compound, separation, relating, the-relating, separate, elements, construct, environment, apprehending.

BUSINESS RELIABILITY

Assurance, salesman, reliability, difference, between, view, dependence, proprietor, what-to-do, in-any, involving, wrong, chief, would-have, decide, in-accordance, path, smoother-than, easier, establishing, to-follow, intricate, chicanery, secretly, accumulating, capital, tangible.

Herbert G. Stockwell **(414)**

Inventory, scarcely, patiently, day-by-day, adhere, simple, who-was, of-reliability, agrees-to, risen, rapidly, of-national, how-did, I-didn't, study, president, intended, humorous, contained, germ, who-would-advance, basic, to-observe, priceless, possessions, unpurchasable.

MODERN COMMERCIAL PUBLICITY

Mightiest, factor, evolution, industrial, business-builder, potency, drummer, mere, positive, creative, grass, grow, grew, multiplies, timorous, hesitating, possessing-the, under-former, get-along, normal, family, merchandising, bounded, meager, deemed, the-luxuries.

Truman A. DeWeese (386)

Fascinating, diverting, to-pull, unprogressive, competitors, psychological, economical, gradually, implants, multiplied, mentalities, enlarges, expands, horizon, designed, convenience, he-would-have-been, blissful, reiteration, so-called, arguments, convinces, wears, constructed, appreciably.

SPEED STUDY XXVI

THE COMMONEST SURNAMES

The commonest surnames given below have been compiled from the list of the commonest surnames found in the cities of New York, Chicago, Philadelphia, Boston, and in England, Wales, and Scotland, as published in the World Almanac. For the method of making distinctions in the spelling of "Mc" and "Mac" see paragraph 116 of the Gregg Shorthand Manual.

1

2

3

4

5

6

7

8

9

10

11

12

13

14

15

16

17

KEY TO THE COMMONEST NAMES

Key: (1) Adams, Allen, Anderson, Baker, Barry, Becker, Bell, Bennett, Boyle, Brady, (2) Brennan, Brown, Burke, Burns, Byrne, Callaghan, Cameron, Campbell, Carroll, (3) Carter, Clarke, Cohen, Cohn, Collins, Connell, Connolly, Connor, Cook, (4) Cooper, Crowley, Daly, Davidson, Davies, Davis, Doherty, Donovan, Doyle, (5) Driscoll, Duffy, Duncan, Dunne, Edwards, Evans, Farrell, Ferguson, Fisher, Fitzgerald, (6) Flynn, Foley, Fox, Fraser, Gallagher, Gordon, Graham, Grant, (7) Gray, Green, Griffiths, Hall, Hamilton, Hanson, Harris, Harrison, Healy, (8) Henderson, Hill, Hoffman, Hughes, Hunter, Jackson, James, Johnson, Johnston, Jones, Kelley, (9) Kelly, Kennedy, Kerr, King, Klein, Larsen, Lee, Levy, Lewis, (10) Lynch, Mahoney, Mahony, Martin, McCarthy, McDonald, McIntosh, McKay, (11) McKenzie, McLean, McLeod, Meyer, Miller, Mitchell, Moore, Morgan, (12) Morris, Morrison, Morse, Munro, Murphy, Murray, Myers, Nolan, (13) O'Brien, O'Connor, O'Donnell, Olsen, Olson, O'Neill, Parker, Paterson, Petersen, (14) Peterson, Phillips, Price, Quinn, Reid, Reilly, Roberts, Robertson, Robinson, Rogers, Ross, (15) Russell, Ryan, Schmidt, Schneider, Scott, Shaw, Shea, Simpson, Sinclair, Smith, (16) Snyder, Stevens, Stewart, Sullivan, Taylor, Thomas, Thompson, Thomson, Turner, (17) Walker, Walsh, Ward, Watson, White, Williams, Wilson, Wood, Wright, Young.

BUSINESS LETTERS

162.

Mason, Easton, fortunes, that-have-been, are-being, cities, retail, for-yourselves, exclusively, prohibitive, worked, advertising-department, skill, prominent, of-its, anticipate, are-you, buyers, stoves, ranges, at-once, give-us, in-knowing.

(262)

163.

Do-this, for-us, rather, do-it, dollars-and-cents, it-does, Hammond, Madison, we-think, the-work, we-can-find, trying, while, and-know, you-are-buying, employ, he-can-do, why-do-you, of-employees, fitness, piece-workers, eliminated, specimen, mediocre, random, reveals, answers.

(273)

164. 245 32

Tests, purposely, difficult, if-they-were, could-not-be, rated, should-be-done, explanation, for-examination, if-you-don't, Harold, Kimball, Wabash-Avenue, why-don't-you, sun, bloom, you-deserve, comforts, wouldn't, oasis, Dixie, Land, make-up, your-mind, route, scenic.

10:25 ... 15 ... 8 ... 11:30 ... 7:30 ... (264)

165.

Homelike, Pullmans, coaches, Flier, leaves, Dearborn, p. m., arrives, year-round, prefer, on-the-road, is-the-only, next-day, over-remembering-that, we-have-set, to-merit, compartments, lower, berths, on-both, dining, Horatio, Fairbanks, Baker, Business-College, Covington, in-a-few-days.

(263)

They-have-been, encouragement, shorthand-work, graduates, multitude, to-lose, continuing, Gregg-Writer, shorthand-writers, on-them, remind, enthusiasm, material, pupils, every-one-of-them, subscriptions, expire, subscribe, school, blanks.

166.

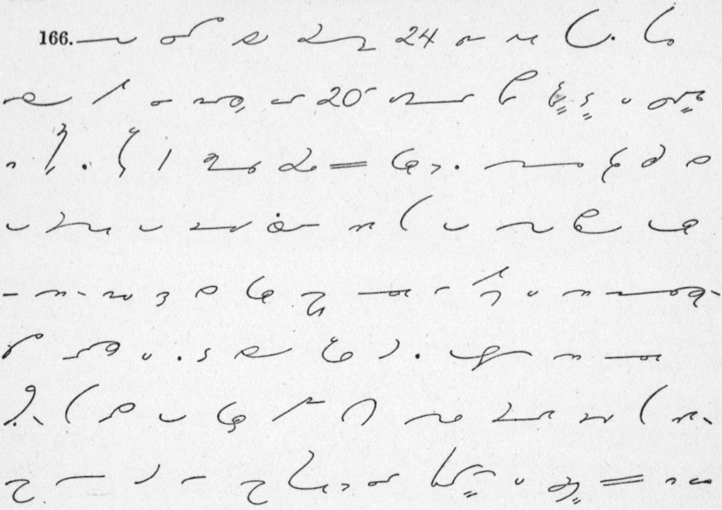

Anthony, Ferguson, Trust, Berkeley, Accountancy, we-wish-to-meet, fairly, higher-than, in-many-cases, in-the-case, from-those, compare, Jordan-Company, San-Francisco, since-that-time, Castner, Becker, Sonora, expansibility, emergency.

(270)

167.— 879

Clothing, as-your's, automatically, bookkeeping, installing-the, opens, awaiting-your-reply, Dougherty, Main, Youngstown, we-are-referring, recent-letters, Acme, we-realize, you-have-not, believing, to-give-us, largest, varnish, goods, in-the-past, again-and-again.

(275)

168.

Prestige, reputation, instilling, ever-widening, circle, customers, methods, line, well-known, familiar, do-not-have, argued, centers-on, producing, specialties, coupled, dealer, to-investigate, Yours-very-sincerely, Childs, Atlanta, definition, historian, achievements, if-so.

(259)

Recognize, confronting, rejection, to-pick, vivid, compressed, events, judged, standards, Short-History, England, omits, reveals, well-balanced, intensely, author, admirable, historians-of-the-country, conspicuous, why-not, write-us, text.

DEAD WORK

Universal, optical, illusion, with-reference, conscious, tasks, sees, inclined, exaggerate, vocation, to-envy, apparently, happier, you-sit, piano, sweeps, onto-the, bosom, of-melody, silence, storm, applause, exclaiming, defined, and-nights, consecrated, toil, dissipation, pleasures, as-their, artist.

Mastery, technique, seems-to-be-done, has-been, invariably, exhausting, intensity, lifetime, apparent, lottery, serious, earned, you-do-not-know, aright, wits, loses, slower, ungifted, plodder, it-is-said, Euclid, formulator, earliest, sciences, geometry, occasion, he-was, Egypt, axiom, proposition.

Edward Howard Griggs (508)

REPORTORIAL EXPERIENCES

18

Restless, indignant, slave, responded, universalize, highway, tollgates, consistent, I-went, House-of-Commons, parliamentary, boy, under-circumstances, successors, adequate, transcribed, printer, strictest, would-have-been, severely, compromising, dark, lantern, post-chaise, galloping.

Strolled, Castle, identify, spot, Russell, vagabonds, pelting, good-natured, colleagues, pocket, handkerchief, canopy, ecclesiastical, procession, excited, political, London, upset, belated, miry, forty-or-fifty, wheelless, drunken, post-boys, Scotch, ladies-and-gentlemen, trivial, fascination.

Charles Dickens (502)

THE FEELING FOR LITERATURE

Dexterity, breast, cunning, retained, resume, very-little, worse, disuse, I-sit, phenomenon, beguile, tedium, mentally, following-the, speaker, finger, tablecloth, imaginary, accept, undying, taken-up, to-night, fruitful, of-myself, injustice, majority, who-read, awakened.

Brightness, novelty, charm, narrative, finds, in-these-things, the-kind, stock, refreshes, introducing, objects, refining, ways, and-with, different, Shakespeare's, historical, skillful, excites, distinct, from-such, refreshment, statesman, confessed, periods, history, enrichment, tumultuous, throbs.

Susceptible, cultivation, responds, noble, essentially, strengthened, sensitive, responsive, contact, with-those, specific, cultivation-of-the-feeling, of-any-kind, geologies, zoology, landscapes, birds, mood, spiritual, cognizance, resource, quickened, nourished, intimacy, delight.

Hamilton Wright Mabie (507)

THE POWER OF IDEAS

Preserves, influences, taste, trustworthy, unconsciously, instinctive, discerning, time, to-cast, purpose, infrequently, stripped, accessories, incidents, network, insistent, persistent, accidents, which-make, worldly, dishonor, injustice, nobility, and-meanness, thinketh, of-what.

Wisdom, persistence, resolution, plastic, stuff, great-men, mold, to-marshal, weapon, to-conquer, adverse, circumstance, group, the-only, statement, doing-the, world's, history, consequences, inspiration, earlier, it-is-only, exchange, clarified, purged.

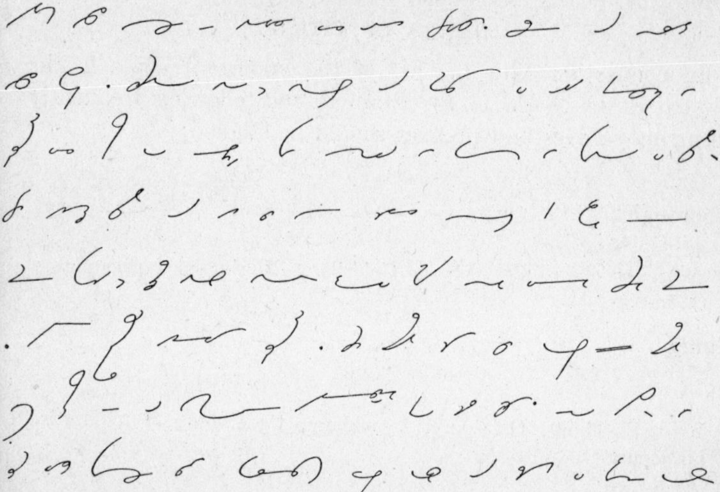

Ernest Fox Nichols (539)

Trustworthiness, painstaking, approach, which-make-up, civilization, progress, to-conceive, gulf, separates, brute, dumb, savagery, to-modern, events, dominions, widening, primitive, origin, spoken, expression, to-another, accelerated, distribution, possessions.

SPEED STUDY XXVII

NAMES OF CITIES

In connection with the list of the important cities in the United States given in the Manual, the following frequently recurring suffixes and prefixes should be studied:

–borough:

Key: Attleboro, Brattleboro, Goldsboro, Hillsboro, Marlborough, Owensboro.

–burg:

Key: Fitchburg, Galesburg, Lynchburg, Ogdensburg, Pittsburgh, Plattsburg.

–bury:

Key: Amesbury, Danbury, Fairbury, Salisbury, Sunbury, Waterbury

–chester:

Key: Baychester, Colchester, Manchester, Portchester, Eastchester, Winchester, Dorchester.

–field:

Key: Clearfield, Fairfield, Mansfield, Pittsfield, Plainfield, Springfield, Wakefield, Winfield.

–ford:

Key: Bedford, Bradford, Hartford, Rockford, Stamford, Stratford, Weatherford.

Fort (*-fort*):

Key: Ft. Collins, Ft. Dodge, Frankfort, Ft. Madison, Ft. Worth, Ft. Wayne.

Grand:

Key: Grand Haven, Grand Island, Grand Junction, Grand Rapids, Grandview.

-ington:

Key: Bloomington, Burlington, Huntington, Stonington, Torrington, Kensington.

New:

Key: New Albany, New Bedford, Newbern, New Britain, New Haven, New London, New Orleans.

Note: In some names it is easier to insert the vowel in "new":

Key: New Castle, New Milford, Newark, Newton.

-port:

Key: Bridgeport, Davenport, Glassport, Lockport, Logansport, Williamsport.

Saint (*St.*):

Key: St. Albans, St. Augustine, St. Charles, St. Joseph, St. Louis, St. Lawrence.

San:

Key: San Angelo, San Antonio, San Bernardino, San Diego, San Francisco, San Juan, San Rafael.

Santa:

Key: Santa Barbara, Santa Cruz, Santa Fe, Santa Rosa.

–son:

Key: Atchison, Henderson, Hudson, Hutchinson, Jackson, Madison, Tucson.

–ton:

Key: Anniston, Brockton, Charleston, Dayton, Evanston, Galveston.

–town:

Key: Charlestown, Georgetown, Jamestown, Johnstown, Morristown, Tarrytown, Watertown.

–ville:

Key: Belleville, Crawfordsville, Danville, Jacksonville, Leadville, Louisville.

–worth:

Key: Ainsworth, Ellsworth, Kenilworth, Leavenworth, Longworth, Wentworth.

BUSINESS LETTERS

169.

Francis, Winslow, St. Louis-Missouri, average, on-the-part, salesman, proves, bigger-than, great-deal, to-sell, still, who-meets, halfway, treats, courteously, scholar, judge, clothes, he-is-not, multiply, tried, persuaded, into-his.

(340)

170. 625 10 40

Has-done, acquainted, he-intended, to-buy, failing, to-make-the, don't-forget, solicited, pestered, patronage, as-you-know, well-enough, and-notice, except-that, waited, attended, Eugene, Spalding, Brush, Detroit-Michigan, logged, southwestern, settlers, tracts, ranging, suitable, grazing.

Roughness-of-the-surface, both, clay, loam, which-will-make, first-class, agricultural, accessible, schools, running, one-to-six, map, colored, logged-off, located, partly, cultivation, adapted, paid, ten-years, together-with, at-the-rate, at-any-time, maturity.

(305)

171.

Complete, descriptions, let-us-know, buy, farming, pieces, corresponding, Clarence, Sterns, Church, Louisville, Kentucky, contracts, great-many-other, Twain's, Authorized, edition, longer, expiring, to-raise, raw, the-low.

(312)

172. 1062

Exhausted, American, must-have, as-well, will-you, everything, expensive, beautifully, easy, ten-days', approval, payments, under-no, no-money, how-long, will-last, Conrad, Olson, Lighting, Fixture, prompt-attention, appreciated, helpful, selections.

Based, fact-that, choosing, fixtures, artistic, comfort, cosy, appearance, usefulness, to-install, tell, enables, purchaser, who-have-the, equipment, scientific, accessories, workmanship, management, from-the-time, shops, assured, expenses, bothers.

(355)

173.

Interference, quietly, merits, it-will-serve, outlay, experts, sketches, Barrett, Euclid-Avenue, Cleveland, consulted, who-are, they-are-of-the-opinion, you-would-find, field, proposed, Hayden-Company, which-has, Weldon, within-a-few-hours.

(355)

They-have-had, labor, conservatively, as-much-as, it-would, or-say, thought, tobacco, center-and-there-are, warehouses, vacated, instances, few, repairs, transformed, very-satisfactory, if-you-will-write-me, of-inspection, if-you-would-like-to-have.

THE SKYSCRAPER

Unceasingly, wagon-loads, dragged, stifling, caissons, concrete, roots, tied, columns, stretched, pierced, a-hundred, sprouting, shoots, crossbeams, lattice, substructure, uproar, vibration, angry, clatter, pneumatic, riveters, shattering, reverberation, incredible, rapidity.

Topmost, derricks, crouched, giant, spiders, braced, post, I-beam, casting-their, softly, tons, girders, turning, against-the, black, surged, prison, bars, I-saw, blue, harbor, miracle, swing, bolted, heavily, towers, clambered, sure-footed, beetles, empty, hung, void, clung, pounded.

Joseph Husband (444)

WHAT IS EFFICIENCY?

Red-hot, rivets, clattering, slim-spun, swung, inaccessible, platforms, glow, forges, blinked, I-am-thinking, slide-rules, grimy, mystic, precision, hairbreadth, I-talked, highest-salaried, goal, ahead, multimillionaire, outrun, rival, of-his-own.

Obscurity, weakness, disease, death, despair, conquers, fate, every-man's, life, possession, forces, one-side, the-other, marshaled, under-efficiency's, banner, assailed, dismembered, realm, choice, changing-us, automatons, provides, hewing, how-much-time, faith, you-could-have, short-cut.

Showing-us, similarly, it-is-not, motion-study, cost-saving, any-other, mechanical, to-reduce, panic, so-much-that, wear, self-management, oil, wisely, rust, to-gather, nerves, wild, is-the-only, one-hundred-million-dollars, ineffective, advertising, three-million-people, somewhere.

Edward E. Purinton **(473)**

THE DISCIPLINE OF THE TIME SCHEDULE

Alexander, Dumas, novels, Monte, Cristo, episode, improbability, Italy, breakfast, Paris, three-months, guests, assembled, skeptical, mysterious, Count, impatient, host, leeway, to-strike, expectation, sinks, zero, suddenly, immaculately, punctuality, politeness, kings, travelers.

. Started, stage-of-the-journey, dependent, sequence, arbitrariness, unstandardized, sweep, thousand-mile, fraction, if-there-are, delays, grumble, mightily, rebates, institution, schedules, mightier-than, benefited, Mississippi, Missouri, steamboat, content, idling, levy, whittling.

Harrington Emerson (475)

THE IMPORTANCE OF THE PRINCIPLES

Deep, bellow, whistle, or-night, sleepy, awakened, prodigious, spasmodic, activity, to-sleep, conducted, when-they-were, crops, houses, watches, schedule, became, definite, regulating, even, who-never, traveled, stenographers, unhesitatingly.

Court, reporting, immediately, transcribing-the, fresh, six-months, theoretically, you-have-nothing, to-guide, arbitrary, changed, with-reference-to-those, transcription, conform, you-are-making, mistake, spending, earnestly, to-perfect, laying-the, genuine, attained.

Frederick H. Gurtler (475)

To-pursue, cheapest, proficient, medicine, architecture, reporters, the-lawyer, to-study, they-must-have, deal, ordinary, spur-of-the-moment, spontaneously, unthinkingly, he-must-be-able, as-the-result, electrician, surgeon, chemist, specialist.

SPEED STUDY XXVIII

CANADIAN NAMES

Key: (1) Toronto, Winnipeg, Montreal, Quebec, Hamilton, Ottawa, London, Victoria, Halifax, (2) Kingston, Brantford, Guelph, St. Thomas, Belleville, Peterborough, Stratford, St. Catharines, Chatham, (3) Brockville, Woodstock, Galt, Owen Sound, Kitchener, Cornwall, Sarnia, Lindsay, Barrie, (4) Collingwood, Cobourg, Orillia, Pembroke, Trenton, Petrolia, Ingersoll, Dartmouth, (5) Yarmouth, Truro, Moncton, St. Johns, Fredericton, Charlottetown, Brandon, Regina, British Columbia, (6) Edmonton, Prince Edward Island, Nova Scotia, New Brunswick, Quebec, Ontario, Manitoba, Assiniboia, Saskatchewan, Alberta, Yukon.

FOREIGN NAMES

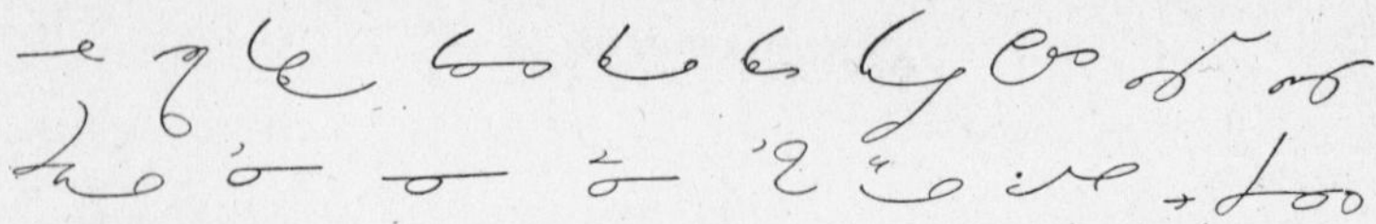

Key: (1) Great Britain, Great Britain and Ireland, United Kingdom, England, Scotland, Ireland, Wales, France, Switzerland, Germany, Belgium, (2) Austria, Holland, Netherlands, Italy, Spain, Portugal, Norway, Sweden, Denmark, Hungary, (3) Russia, Turkey, Greece, Roumania, Persia, India, China, Japan, Palestine, Syria, Egypt, (4) Siam, Korea, Morocco, Tunis, Transvaal, Natal, Burma, Tripoli, Sudan, (5) Mexico, Cuba, Brazil, Panama, Chile, Peru, Bolivia, Argentina, Ecuador, Yucàtan, (6) Venezuela, South America, North America, Central America, South Africa, Australia, Honduras, New Zealand, Jamaica.

IMPORTANT FOREIGN CITIES

Key: (1) Amsterdam, Antwerp, Barcelona, Belfast, Birmingham, Bombay, Bordeaux, Bremen, (2) Breslau, Bristol, Brussels, Budapest, Canton, Cologne, Copenhagen, Dresden, (3) Dublin, Edinburgh, Florence, Genoa, Glasgow, Hamburg, Havana, Havre, Lisbon, (4) Liverpool, Lyons, Madrid, Manchester, Marseilles, Melbourne, Milan, (5) Munich, Naples, Nottingham, Odessa, Peking, Plymouth, Portsmouth, Santiago, (6) Shanghai, Southampton, Stockholm, Sydney, Trieste, Valparaiso, Yokohama, Zurich.

BUSINESS LETTERS

174.

Construction-Company, Scranton, insistent, Grain, Elevator, we-understand, at-length, we-can-do, in-the-way, assuring-you, we-have-made, big, Galveston, extensively, Engineering, Record, which-has-been, owners, of-this-character, is-going, impressive, it-is-certain, exploit.

(322)

175.

We-think-it-is, distinctive, in-the-long, it-may-be, consisting, December, closing, Quinn, Emerson, Nashville, Forward, schoolmen, all-over-the-country, nobody, when-they-will, extremely, unsettled, over-producing, prepaid, express.

Of-name, and-such, column, check, with-order, during-the-past, it-is-only, spreading-the, expense, desirability, prolonging-your, registrations, it-is-certainly, in-a-few-days, quickest, that-come, two-or-three, from-now, unavoidably, with-other, to-print, and-see.

(331)

176.

Reach-you, cordially-yours, Amos, Howells, Front, Street, Newport, standardized, discounts, minds-of-the-public, to-disturb, radical, policy, sentimental, good-many-years, increases, temporarily, for-the, as-to-have, curtailment, production, imperative, dependable, wall.

(331)

177.

Finish, tangible, contrast, effective, will-make, prospective, builders, users, displayed, Alabastine, be-sure-that, alert, to-talk, to-recommend, unusual, Printers', Publishing-Company, affords, each-number, library, marking, staff, many other, jobbers.

February, commenting, Postmaster-General, one-cent, insufficient, distributing, sender, directions, finding-the, addressee, emphasize, clerical, imposition, penalty, offender, thoroughness, the-trouble, locally, Department, receives, two-cents, somewhat, diluted, negligent, properly, careless.

(358)

178.

Round, figure, inducement, scrimping, addressing-departments, envelopes, omitting, streets, advocate, postage, protest, I-ask-you, Michael, O'Hara, Avenue, New-Bedford, Aeolian, ought-to-know, phonograph, box, chamber, tone, shading, technicalities, convey, impression.

(312)

Selecting, style, believe, greatest, lose, sight-of-the-fact-that, musical, instrument, twofold, gift, family, permanence, whoever, standpoint, cabinet, that-these, noted, period, showrooms, finer, appropriate, music, that-will, harmony.

INDEPENDENCE DAY ADDRESS

Consist, declarations, translation, adopted, terms, of-our-own, condition, lives, democracy, themselves, moral, tribunal, and-therefore, awakened, inspiring, the-original, fountain, of-liberty, independence, America, drafts, patriotic, to-renew.

Veins, to-feel, lonely, people-of-the-United-States, dream, more-and-more, will-bring, youth, renewal, enterprise, inconsistent, human-rights, above-all, exalted, sympathy, thrills, politic, I-don't-know, that-there, grievances, of-mankind.

Woodrow Wilson (482)

THE STORY OF ELECTRICAL WIRE

Document, lifted, shine, unto, guide, justice, electrical, pounds, aluminum, sizes, wire, every-year, some-of-these, as-large-as, wrist, a-million-feet, twenty-five-pounds, insulated, telephone, telegraph, ocean, cable, steel, converted, yearly, excavations, ornaments, ancients.

To-beat, thin, sheets, strips, rounded, hammering, filing, century, die, plate, in-the-latter, to-operate, invention, introduced, unimportant, varied, processes, of-manufacture, heated, revolving, rolls, reducing, diameter, depending, coils.

Popular Electricity (502)

Dipped, acid, to-remove, loose, lubricant, pulling, decreasing, drilled, particles, strained, elongated, harder, brittle, repeated, annealings, drawings, this-may-be-done, originally, four-inches, four-feet, thousandth, extended, miles, length, discarded, diamonds, dies, fractional, striking.

PRACTICE FROM ACTUAL SPEAKING

At-best, mimicry, lack, imitates, judiciously, managed, prepare, effectually, monotone, has-reached, accustom, cadence, rises, falls, rushes, pauses, voices, tones, articulations, especially, utterance, which-does-not, humor, shortcomings, sermons, lectures, prentice, chosen.

Slow, ministers, Gospel, lawyers, rostrum, orators, bona-fide, practitioner, overtax, speakers, fast, borne, straining, to-keep, except, occasional, spurts, discouragingly, lurch, often, successfully, sermon, address, passages, peroration, warming, subject, beyond-his, despond, as-soon-as-the.

David Wolfe Brown (508)

CONCENTRATION

Pencil, cool, legible, clauses, of-minor, in-both, stages, young, upon-any, court-room, of-legal, Carlyle, weakest, creature, single, accomplish, whereas, dispersing-his, over-many, unwavering, sacrificed, conflicting, ambitions, specialized, intensive, purposeful.

This-does-not, one-sided, capable, broad, faceted, mentality, concentrated, who-knows, goal, focusing, in-this-world, concentration, dominated, directed, weaknesses, he-may-have, concentrate, force, vigor, on-the-whole, centralize, brain.

Orison Swett Marden (470)

Executes, elephant, pick, pin, uproot, trunk, throughout, body, to-manipulate, infinitely, scattered, explosives, thimbleful, powder, behind, rifle, cartload, poorest, outstrips, class, leader, eminent, discoverers, inventors, red-letter, owed, distinction, of-intense.

SPEED STUDY XXIX

RAILWAY PHRASES

Assistant (prefix)
Agent (suffix):

Key: advertising agent, claim agent, purchasing agent, assistant purchasing agent.

Auditor:

Key: assistant auditor, ticket auditor, freight auditor, passenger auditor.

Note: It will be readily seen that the joining of a vowel to a single stroke would give the appearance of one word, therefore disjoin the second word in such cases—as in "freight agent." When another letter is added, as in "general freight agent," the vowel is joined because the form is absolutely distinctive.

Baggage:

Key: baggage master, baggage agent, baggage department, baggage check.

Chief:

Key: chief clerk, chief draftsman, chief engineer, chief counsel.

Division:

Key: western division, southern division, eastern division, central division.

Engineer:

Key: engineer of construction, civil engineer, mechanical engineer, electrical engineer, locomotive engineer.

Freight:

Key: freight agent, freight auditor, freight claim auditor, freight claim agent, freight engineer, freight car.

General:

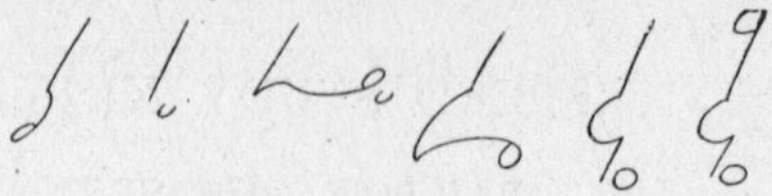

Key: general freight agent, general auditor, general claim auditor, general baggage agent, general purchasing agent, assistant general purchasing agent.

Manager:

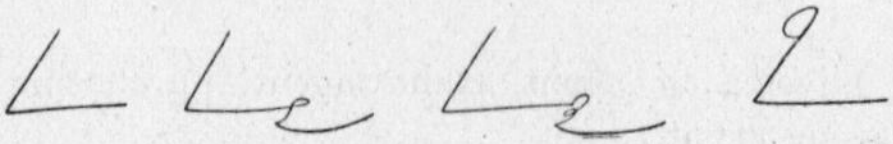

Key: general manager, general manager eastern lines, general manager western lines, assistant general manager.

Mechanical:

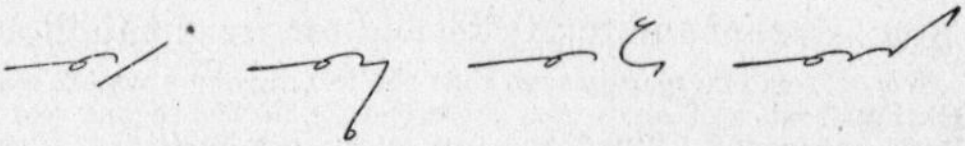

Key: mechanical department, mechanical engineer, mechanical operation, mechanical condition.

Passenger:

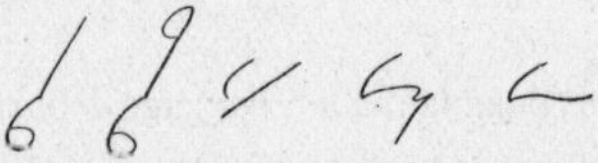

Key: general passenger agent, assistant general passenger agent, passenger department, passenger coach, passenger car.

Superintendent:

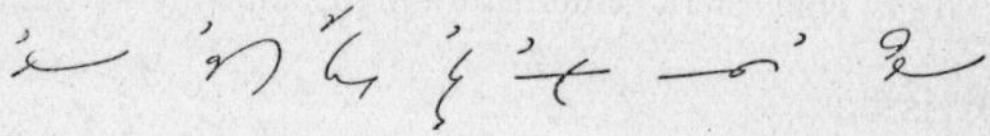

Key: superintendent of telegraph, superintendent of the eastern division, superintendent of transportation, superintendent of shops, superintendent of motive power, mechanical superintendent, assistant superintendent of telegraph.

Ticket:

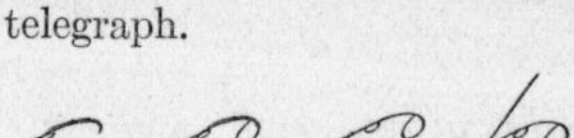

Key: ticket auditor, ticket agent, assistant ticket agent, general ticket agent.

Traffic:

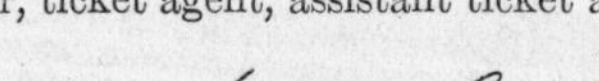

Key: traffic manager, passenger traffic manager, assistant passenger traffic manager.

BUSINESS LETTERS

179.

Rupert, Van Dyke, Liberty, Evansville, Indiana, Commodore, William, Hale, Thompson, resort, pleasurable, bounce, over-bumps, tires, swallow, dust, perspective, bunks, lockers, chairs, to-move, Fay, Bowen, drives, hour-after-hour, clean, throttle, spark.

Steering, wheel, you-feel, monarch, as-you, skim, waves, limitations, inclinations, cruises, to-any, destination, dictated, Michigan-City, the-river, Lockport, canal, Wilmette, municipal, pier, mooring, picnic, supper, point-of-view, broader, inland, parting, to-my-mind, stanchest.

(478)

180.

Extra-strong, mahogany, upper, interior, slack, Christmas, drop, any-time, Bonaparte, Washington-D. C., Gary, Frick, on-behalf-of-the-steel, I-have-not-been, assets, majority-of-the-securities, as-the-only, avoiding, transaction, to-purchase.

They-would-not, that-they-are-aware, attack, prevent, recklessly, untruthfully, as-a-matter-of-fact, to-decline, persevered, several-years, accusations, slightly, so-that-it-is, immensely, seems-the, fitted, break, ruinous.

(445)

181.—

Urged, upon-them, bankers, who-are-now, asserted, ought-not, to-take-the, I-felt, interpose, objections, Silas, Woodbury, Editor-of-the-Farm, Journal, Malden, shortage, October, November, approximately, fertilizers, in-the-past, congested, require, railroad, products.

Moving-the, short-period, as-they-have-been, in-past, years, co-operation-of-the-farmers, is-necessary, relieve, extend, the-length, maximum, as-possible, foodstuffs, and-larger, one-of-the, unloaded, several-times, hauls.

(539)

Supply, bigger, investment, farmer, food, starts, in-many, sections, to-haul, snow, bad, break-up, least, rushing, costs, lowest, profitable, editorially, columns, freight, the-danger, of-embargo, advisability, we-feel, to-them, concerned.

THE SPIRIT OF LOYALTY

Policy, house, motive, fixing, on-our, let-us, deep, it-may-be, worthy, we-don't, tire, wastes, and-energy, we-are-prepared, spend, leisure, upon-your, golf, contact, with-people, you-would-like-to-know, vital, effort, interested, aptitude, you-have-gone, you-can-make, anything-else.

Do-you-think, you're, salesmánship, who-are-making, extra-money, to-know, about-your, in-other-words, loyal, spirit, exclusiveness, which-makes, pursuit, suspicious, who-is-not, that-is-said, has-given, master, gardener, I-like, brains, capacity, on-the-right, to-developing.

E. St. Elmo Lewis (659)

Industrious, the-things, he-knows, somebody, he-thinks, it-will-pay, self-respect, moment, somebody-else, he-do-things, appearances, polite, punctual, reticent, wellsprings, of-his-own, impulses, in-themselves, apart, may-not-be, guiding, that-makes, sticks, fable, personality.

THE SERVICE OF BUSINESS SCHOOLS

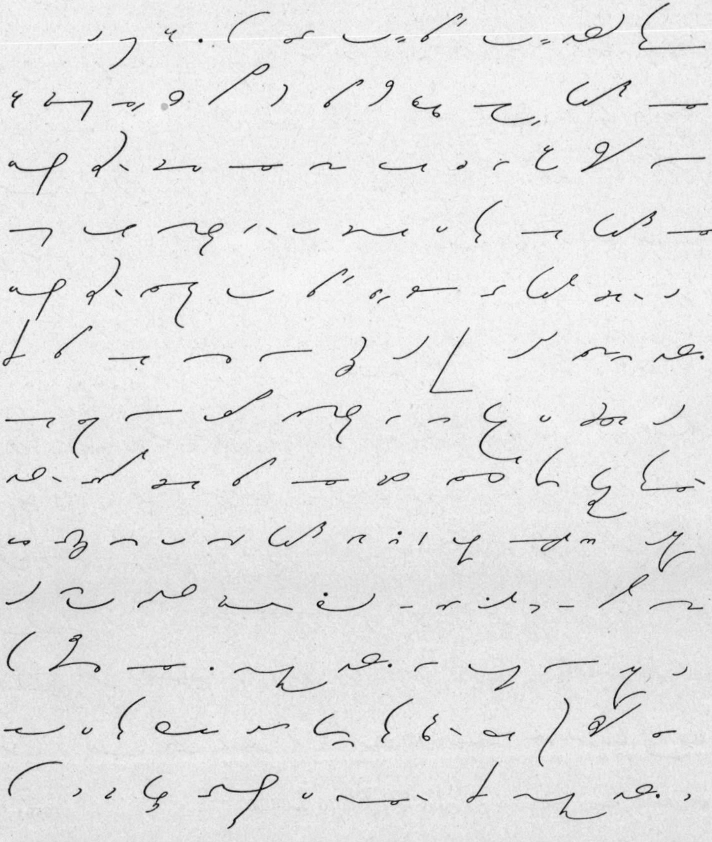

Well-educated, seriously, produces, vision, small, afforded, they-must-be, term, foresight, technical, training, readily, to-grasp, professional, marts-of-the-world, and-obtain, so-long, held, we-have-given, cultural, knowledge, experience, wasted.

Indispensable, supplemented, laboratory, just-as, science, greatly, this-can-be, earning-the, have-never, epoch-making, attaining-the, European, War, reciprocity, consequent, specialists, with-such, in-particular, furthering, disregarded.

Duties, to-perform, study, research, students, peculiar, geography, languages, carry, commerce, conception, of-nations, familiarity, supplied, need-not, in-this-connection, phase, we-might-be. tempted, overlook, I-refer, exert.

James C. Egbert (700)

PREPAREDNESS IN BUSINESS

I-do-not, restrict, commonly, presupposed, of-learning, in-business, uncertain, unduly, prevalent, hence, topic, enlargement, readiness, of-new, at-home, statistical, analyses, concerning, anticipation, of-needs, engrossed, nowadays.

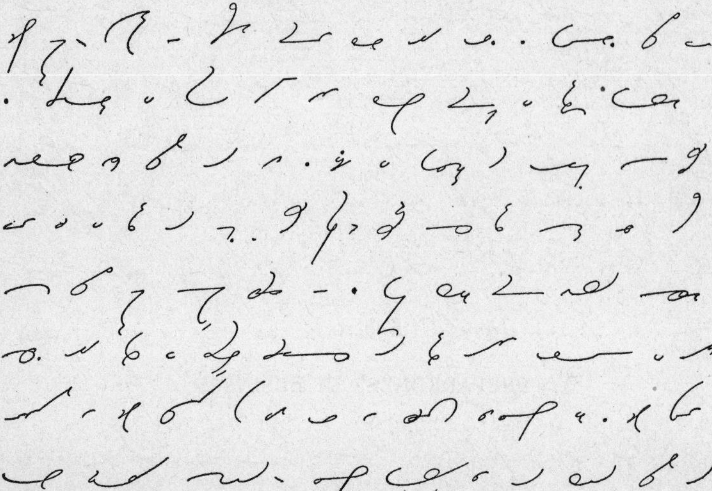

Stage, promising, generalization, elaborate, formulation, to-realize, launching, safely, sea, voyage, embodied, project, arose, minds, carrying, verified, intuition, imagination, played, ultimately, flamed, consciousness, originators, testify, operate, Newton, stupendous, leap, hints, stars.

As-they-are, state-of-mind, comparing, passion, afield, relevant, experiences, nimble, intellectual, launch, boldly, speculation, open-minded, struggling, preconceptions, imperfect, to-welcome, title, despite, impact, cherished, leaven, fermenting, evolving, tool.

John Calder (719)

Shelf, Socrates, dawn, attitude-of-the-mind, decisions, habitually, to-observe, describe, classify, phenomena, interpretative, solely, outstanding, inception, operating-departments, storehouses, conveyors, in-this-matter, distinguishes, statistician, planner.

SPEED STUDY XXX

Common Expressions in Business Letters. — The business expressions treated in this Study are not such as will be approved by the best writers on English, or by the correspondents of the most progressive business houses. Hackneyed, machine-made, uninteresting, and oftentimes meaningless, they belong to a past age. They *should* not be used, but they *are* used. But we must face conditions as they are, not as we should like to arrange them, and since they are the "business English" of ninety-five per cent of the business offices, they properly come within the sphere of our study.

These introductory and closing expressions, being set forms, are usually dictated very rapidly, and the stenographer will do well to get a writing acquaintance with them.

COMMON BUSINESS EXPRESSIONS

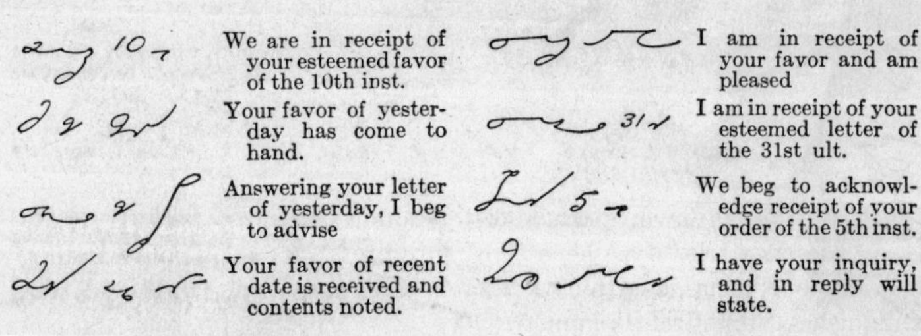

We are in receipt of your esteemed order, which has been carefully noted.

Your favor of the 7th inst. was duly received.

Your postal card is at hand.

Replying to your kind favor of the 3d inst., I would advise that

In reply to yours of yesterday, we have to say

Referring to your letter of the 9th, we beg to say

We duly received your letter of recent date

Your esteemed favor of the 8th inst. is at hand.

Your letter of recent date is received and contents carefully noted.

I have to-day received your kind favor.

Your favor of this morning to hand and noted.

Your communication of the 5th is before us.

and oblige Yours truly,

greatly oblige Yours respectfully,

Thanking you for the order,

Thanking you for your order,

Thanking you for the favor, we beg to remain

Thanking you for your kind attention to the matter,

Hoping to hear from you again at an early date,

Let us hear from you by return mail.

and assuring you of our best attention at all times,

Your immediate attention will oblige Yours respectfully,

With kind regards and best wishes,

Trusting this will be entirely satisfactory to you,

at as early a date as possible, we are Yours truly,

as soon as possible, we remain Cordially yours,

Thanking you in advance, and with kind personal regards,

Thanking you for your careful attention in the matter,

and expecting to hear from you in the course of a few days,

Awaiting your reply, I remain Sincerely yours,

and hoping to see you in our office in the near future,

and regretting that we are unable,

PRESIDENT WILSON'S WAR MESSAGE

Delivered at a Joint Session of the Two Houses of Congress, April 2, 1917

Congress, extraordinary, session, constitutionally, permissible, the-responsibility, officially, first-day, restraints, submarines, to-sink, sought, Great-Britain-and-Ireland, western, coasts, Europe, enemies, Mediterranean, warfare, commanders, conformity, passenger, boats.

Vessels, destroy, resistance, escape, attempted, to-save, meager, haphazard, distressing, instance-after-instance, cruel, unmanly, swept, restriction, flag, cargo, errand, ruthlessly, and-without, mercy, neutrals, belligerents, sorely, bereaved, stricken, Belgium, unmistakable, identity, compassion.

Hitherto, subscribed, humane, civilized, dominion, highways, painful, stage-after-stage, accomplished, conscience, retaliation, weapons, winds, scruples, humanity, understandings, intercourse-of-the-world, involved, wanton, destruction, noncombatants, men-women-and-children.

Darkest, of-modern, legitimate, peaceful, innocent, stirred, of-other, neutral, overwhelmed, waters, discrimination, challenge, all-mankind, moderation, counsel, temperateness, befitting, revenge, victorious, assertion, vindication, human-right, champion, that-it-would, suffice.

Unlawful, interference, violence, armed, neutrality, impracticable, outlaws, to-defend, attacks, merchantmen, privateers, cruisers, visible, chase, prudence, grim, dealt, denies, areas-of-the-sea, publicist, intimation, conveyed, guards, pirates, ineffectual, worse-than.

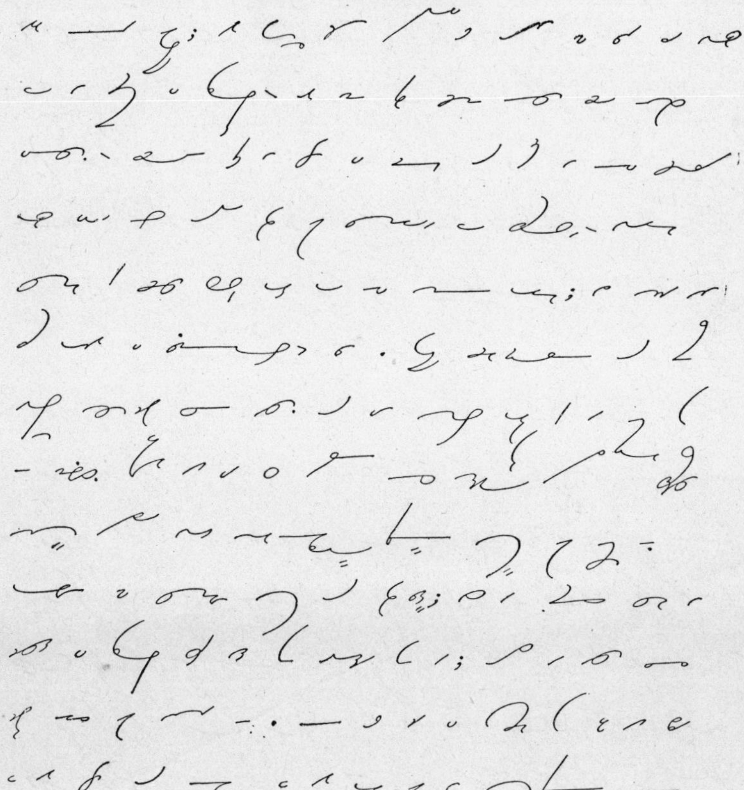

To-prevent, to-draw, effectiveness, incapable, submission, sacred, ignored, violated, array, profound, sense, solemn, tragical, character-of-the-step, involves, unhesitating, obedience, I-advise-that-the, declare, the-recent, course, formally, status, thrust, resources, Empire.

Utmost, incident, extension, credits, so-far-as-possible, mobilization, resources-of-the-country, incidental, equipment-of-the-navy, respects, enemy's, 500,000, who-should, liability, authorization, subsequent, increments, granting, sustained, equitably, generation, taxation.

That-it-would-be, unwise, borrowed, urge, to-protect, our-people, hardships, evils, infliction, vast, measures, interfering, as-little-as-possible, military, in-every-way, I-shall-take-the, departments, committees, I-have-mentioned, I-hope-that, framed, safeguarding-the, directly.

Momentous, the-world, driven, two-months, I-do-not-believe, altered, clouded, by-them, same-things, Senate, January, to-vindicate, in-the-life-of-the-world, selfish, autocratic, amongst, self-governed, henceforth, observance, feasible, we-have-seen.

Beginning, insisted, of-responsibility, citizens, quarrel, towards, it-was-not, entering-this, previous, determined, unhappy, nowhere, provoked, dynasties, ambitious, who-were, fellow-men, pawns, intrigue, posture, under-cover, cunningly, contrived, deception, aggression.

Kept, privacy, guarded, happily, opinion, steadfast, partnership, democratic, covenants, league, vitals, plottings, inner, circles, render, corruption, seated, assurance, heartening, within-the, last-few-weeks, Russia, intimate, relationships.

Attitude, autocracy, crowned, summit, structure, terrible, reality, Russian, shaken, added, majesty, Prussian, unsuspecting, communities, offices, criminal, intrigues, afoot, unity, began, unhappily, conjecture, courts, perilously, disturbing-the, dislocating-the.

Instigation, support, official, accredited, checking-these, extirpate, interpretation, ignorant, entertains, friendship, and-means, to-stir, intercepted, Minister, Mexico, eloquent, evidence, accepting-this, hostile, presence.

To-check, nullify, now-that, veil, ultimate, liberation, included, everywhere, obedience, tested, foundations, conquest, dominion, indemnities, compensation, sacrifices, champions, rights, we-fight, rancor, punctilio, profess, I-have-said, allied.

They-have-not, upon-us, Austro-Hungarian, avowed, unqualified, lawless, disguise, Tarnowski, Ambassador, Austria-Hungary, I-take-the, for-the-present, postponing, discussion, Vienna, enter-this, fairness, animus, enmity, injury, disadvantage, opposition, irresponsible, amuck, let-me-say.

So-much-as-the, re-establishment, of-mutual, for-the-time-being, hearts, bitter, months, patience, forbearance, to-prove, of-men-and-women, and-loyal, Americans, fealty, allegiance, rebuking, restraining-the, who-may-be, disloyalty, repression, countenance, malignant, oppressive.

(3683)

Fiery, to-lead, disastrous, wars, civilization, precious, for-the-things, which-we-have, nearest, democracy, for-the-right, submit, authority, universal, concert, safety, dedicate, our-lives, fortunes, privileged, that-gave, treasured, helping.

100

Muriel A. Beal
+
Muriel D. Gilbert